BEAUTY DELIVERED

NO MORE ADDICTION, NO MORE SHAME

Sonya Rolande

To my King of kings and Lord of lords,

the eternal Lover of my soul, Jesus Christ,

Who redeemed me from all my sins

so that I may have life and have it in abundance!

Thank You for everything!

To my family and my unborn children:

God definitely has His hands upon our lives!

This generational blessing I dedicate to you!

Contents

Acknowledgments

I thank the Lord for the great leaders He placed in my life to mentor me: Pastor Bayo Adewole, Mrs. Gail Ciarrachi, Deaconess Treasure Okenla, Pastor Sola Babalola, and Pastor Raeni Bankole. *May the Lord replenish you for all the seeds you have planted in me! To the glory of God, here is one of the fruits!*

I want to appreciate Dr. Rebecca Brown, Chester and Betsy Kylstra. I praise the Lord for how He used your books and ministries to bless me! *May the Lord continue to take you to greater heights and increase your capacity, in Jesus' name!*

I want to thank my "team of advisors" for *Beauty Delivered*: Drakia Wilkins, Jummy Akosile, Olivia Adesanya, Dami Oyeyipo, Michael Odeniyi, Samuel Paul, and Pastor Wilson Ogbeide. *I truly appreciate your review of the manuscript and continual support! May God forever bless all the works of your hands!*

I want to appreciate my dedicated and very talented editors, Sherilynn Asuoha and Linda Stubblefield. *God knew you were the perfect people to put the finishing touch to this book! May the Lord bring tremendous success to all your ventures and increase your anointing of excellence!*

I want to thank Rotimi Kehinde, CEO of GodKulture, for his professional help with my book cover. *God will continue to enlarge your coast and make your name great!*

Special thanks to my entire church family at Jesus House Chicago! *You have no idea how much God used you to support me when I was writing this book. I will forever remember and cherish your seeds of love in my life.*

My sincere appreciation goes to my parents for the sacrifices and investments they made for my siblings and me. *May the Lord God continue to watch over you and reward you for your labor!* I also want to thank my siblings, Sophya and Daniel, for their love and care for me. *I love you all dearly!*

Foreword

*S*onya is one of the emerging leaders at Jesus House Chicago. Not too long after she joined the church, I could tell that she genuinely loved the Lord. She had a drive that was not moved by sight but by her strong faith in God. In the four years since she has joined the church, she has been a godly example to her generation and a role model to the children with whom she works in our midweek Awana program. Despite the challenges that she has faced in her personal life, she continues to dedicate herself to the work of God, and her dedication is evident by how fast she has risen to the leadership role in Awana Ministry and by her commitment as a part of our Worship and Prayer Ministries.

I was not surprised when she told me about her book as I

knew she had a lot to offer the world. Her manuscript was a delight to read, and it was clear that her transformation was nothing short of a miracle. Her level of transparency and the depth of revelations she obtained from the Lord, while writing *Beauty Delivered*, impressed me. It is worthy of mention that God took Sonya from a place of addiction and bondage, and He redeemed her past by giving her beauty for years of ashes. God is known for using people who might have failed and fallen in the past but are ready to be transparent about their failures. Sonya's testimony is a great portrayal of God's mercy and love for humanity.

Her story is a reminder that it does not matter how bad you have messed up, God is not only able to redeem you but also turn your *mess* into a *message*. *Beauty Delivered* takes you into a wonderful journey of salvation, redemption, deliverance, and discovery of purpose. For anyone who is in any form of oppression from sin, I pray that, through Sonya's story, you will experience God's mighty hand of deliverance. I also pray that *Beauty Delivered* will inspire you to discover and walk according to God's purpose for your life!

– Pastor Bayo Adewole
Senior Pastor, Jesus House Chicago

Introduction

$\mathcal{I}$ was addicted to pornography. Smoking, among other habits, became an obsession of mine. I occupied my life with what was killing me in retaliation to my parents and their decisions, or so I told myself. Shortly after I entered my teen years, my parents decided to divorce. I blamed them for what I had become. Yet, the truth is, I did not understand why I craved the lifestyle I had chosen for myself. Nothing I did ever really satisfied me or made me feel better about what had happened in my life. All I knew for certain was that I was enveloped in darkness.

I can vividly recount my teenage years when I would aimlessly wander the streets of France in the twilight hours with the wrong people, taking part in the wrong activities. My mother would call and search for me—to no avail. All the while, I was busy searching for my identity and approval. In fact, all of my life, before now, I had the burning sensation that I was missing *something*, though I did not know what. I only knew that without that something, I was empty. Because I did not know what I was looking for, I spent countless days and nights filling that emptiness with anyone or anything I could get my hands on. I searched for people and things to complete me, but I remained empty. The inability to find inner peace led me to a life of destruction. At the age of twenty-two, depression found me. I had reached an all-time low, and seemingly, my addictions were no longer able to compensate for what I truly needed. I was bleeding on the inside, and I was desperately in need of a savior.

Whether or not I believed it, God was always there. In fact, Jesus waited patiently for me to let Him into my heart so that He could make me whole. Giving my life to Christ was the best decision I ever made. For the first time in my life, I no longer felt bound but free. God had translated me from the kingdom of darkness to the kingdom of His marvelous light! God was ready to heal every wound of my past and to give me a complete and new life in Him. The past was now the past. I no longer had to feel ashamed or bad for what I had gone through. In Christ, I was now free from condemnation. Jesus had paid the price on the Cross for all of my sins, and He had completely redeemed me.

By allowing Christ into my life, I had accessed the key to my freedom. I spent years being angry at people and life. I recall the many times when I would curse at my parents or even stop talking to family and friends. I was unfulfilled within, and I did everything to cover up my lack of contentedness. I tried to become a better person and to discontinue many of my old addictions, but I could not. On the contrary, I became more and more bitter toward others, life, and even myself. My addictions were only exacerbated, leading to more and greater addictions. From pornography, masturbation, fornication to drinking excessively and smoking, I had reached a dangerous point as an addict. My life was spiraling downward, and I needed a savior to rescue me. I was full of hurt and broken by the mistakes of my past. I had no real life; I was completely dead in my sins.

But God, in His infinite mercy and love toward me, led me to Jesus—the only One who could save me. And God made me alive in Christ. I no longer had to endure the pain and shame of my past. Jesus had already paid the price for all of my wrongs, and He had given me victory over sins. In Him, I had now acquired the power to overcome every of my addictions and break all of the chains that had bound me for years. God was ready to wipe away the tears of my past and give me beauty for ashes!

When I gave my life to Christ, I knew a major transformation had taken place within me, and I truly felt like a new creature in Him. I was becoming more forgiving toward others. I no longer felt the need to chase after that to which I was once addicted. These sinful desires were gone...yet, not completely. I was about to learn that work still needed to be done in me. I was continuing to reap the effects of my past—whether good or bad. Christ had paid the price for all of the sins I ever committed, but I needed to claim my victory in Him and use His power to break free. I realized that unless I prayed away the evil chains of my past, I would still remain in bondage, *enslavement*.

About a year after giving my life to Christ, God took me through a long season of deliverance. He started revealing to me the many doorways of my life that were still opened to the enemy, *Satan the devil*. Through a series of dreams, God opened my spiritual eyes and showed me answers to many issues that I could have never figured out on my own. He gave me revelations about the sins committed by my ancestors and events of my childhood. He also helped me understand how my sexual relationships had created soul ties with others. In fact, God started giving me mastery of how to deliver myself from the bondages of my past.

When I entered this season of deliverance, I had no idea that all of the revelations I received from God were for a definite purpose. I knew from my years of leading a rebellious life and being involved in sexual sins that God wanted to break many chains from my past. Nonetheless, I was yet to learn that God would use me to help others who had gone through similar circumstances. In reality, God did not see my years of living a promiscuous and rebellious life as something to hide but as a platform. Through my own deliverance, God had taught me how to completely break free from many evil afflictions, and He wanted me to share what I had learn with others. God had planned from the beginning to turn my "mess" into a "message". My season of deliverance was all for a purpose, and I was glad that God could use my story for His glory. Yet, this season of deliverance came at a price that I was not ready to pay.

As a young believer, I was totally excited about my new walk with Christ. Everything about life seemed easier. In my relationships, I was becoming a better person to those involved in my life, and I was no longer aggressive toward others like I once was. People could see the change in me, and I rejoiced greatly when I could share with them how God had changed me into a better person. In my career, God had blessed me with a stable and flexible job, which allowed me to launch the business venture I had worked on for years. I really felt that God was on my side, working everything for my good.

Nevertheless, for the first time in my walk with Christ, challenges started to arise. The people I thought were closest to me began to despise and attack me because of my faith. To add, within a year after launching my business, we had to close it down. At the time, I had decided to leave my job to invest all of my time in my business. But when the business closed, I was left with no stable income to support myself. To my surprise, all of these issues started occurring during my season of deliverance, which was now paralleled with a season of financial hardship. Seemingly, the more that I prayed, the more challenges I started to encounter.

I became very angry at God. I could not understand why He was allowing all of these problems to take place in my life. Yet, God had a specific purpose behind it all. God allowed me to go through a difficult season so that He could get me closer to fulfilling His purpose for my life.

Beauty Delivered will take you on a transformational journey in which God turned a lifetime of bondage into beauty. Indeed, Jesus delivered beauty into my life the day I gave my life to Him. Throughout this book, I share with you stories of how I grew in my walk with the Lord, how God healed the wounds that had held me in bondage for years, how God allowed afflictions to shape my character, and how my season of deliverance led me to discover God's purpose for my life. Beauty Delivered bears the testimony that there is nothing God cannot do, and no one God cannot change. May God deliver beauty into your life as you read!

PART ONE

A New Creature in Christ

CHAPTER ONE
Jesus Knocked, & I Opened

"For God so loved the world that He gave His only begotten Son, that whoever believes in Him should not perish but have everlasting life." – John 3:16

At twenty-four years old, I was engrossed in sexual sins and completely addicted to smoking. My life was bound to either men or things. I was madly in love with my then boyfriend. He had become my idol, and I had reached a point where I was willing to give up everything for him.

My boyfriend had Christian friends, and to appease him, I began attending church services with them. I had no plans of giving my life to Jesus. Maybe the smoke was clouding my vision because I did not even notice that Jesus was drawing my heart nearer and nearer to His. I had yet to learn that

God had actually drawn me to church in the first place. I was bound to my worldly life and unwilling to surrender it to Christ. Nevertheless, to the glory of God, the day came when everything turned around. I will never forget the moment when the Holy Spirit[1] convicted me of my sins.

One day a very intense, heated argument with my boyfriend ended in our completely dissolving our relationship. The problem was that I wanted him to do something for me that he refused to do. I had invested so much into our relationship. Whatever he had asked me to do, I did, but I felt my investment was neither reciprocated nor appreciated. I wanted him to complete me. I wanted our relationship to eradicate all of the pain I had endured throughout my lifetime. Yet this young man whom I had idolized and in whom I had placed all of my hope rejected me. When our relationship was over, I had nothing left to fill the holes in my heart. I was left completely broken and in dire need of a savior. I felt very empty on that day—abandoned and hopeless.

From God's perspective, the idol standing between us was finally gone, and then the Holy Spirit gave me a reality check and brought me face to face with myself and my sins. At that moment for the first time in my life, I realized that I was a sinner and that without surrendering my life to Jesus, I had no life at all. I knew that I could no longer lead my life on my own and that I truly had no power of my own. When I was finally able to acknowledge that I was empty without God, I gave it all to Jesus. I told God that I was sorry for all of my sins, and I asked Jesus to come into my heart and be my Lord and Savior. I was broken, and only God could fix my mess.

"If you openly declare that Jesus is Lord and believe in your heart
that God raised him from the dead, you will be saved."

– Romans 10:9, NLT

The decision I made to accept Jesus Christ as my Lord and Savior was the best decision I ever made in my life. On that day, God granted me eternal life and the key to repairing my foundations. A couple days after giving my life to Christ, God led one of my closest friends, who was also a Christian, to give me a book entitled, *Your Knight in Shining Armor* by P.B. Wilson.[2] The purpose of this book was to teach women how to become complete in God. At the beginning of the book, the author encouraged every reader to dedicate six months to God only, without dating anyone. My friend knew the book would be a perfect fit for where I was in my walk with Christ.

My broken relationship with my now ex-boyfriend had led me to give my life to Christ, and I was in desperate need of love. If I did not make this six-month commitment, I would have run into the arms of another man. God wanted me to discover His love toward me so that I would not need anyone else to complete me. What I needed was not another man but God alone. The devastation of my heartbreak had opened a door for God to finally heal me and to deliver beauty into my life.

"Father, I commit the next six months to You for You to heal me from the foundations upward. I will not to date anyone during this time. I surrender all aspects of my life to You, in Jesus' name."

(Psalm 11:3)

A Product of God's Grace

"Though I am the least deserving of all God's people, he graciously gave me the privilege of telling the Gentiles about the endless treasures available to them in Christ." – Ephesians 3:8, NLT

By redeeming me through His Son, Jesus Christ, God showed me that He had mercy on me. God's mercy and underserved grace brought about the miracle of forgiveness into my life. I am a true product of God's grace. Like Paul mentioned in Ephesians 3:8, I knew I was the least deserving of the grace of God. I was the worst amongst sinners. How could I not have been? I used to insult and curse my parents. I knew if many people saw the way I used to treat my parents, especially my mother, they would have easily judged me. I was a very rebellious child and the least likely to ever become a Christian.

I recall a time when I went shoplifting with friends. We all ended up in jail for a night. My mother was extremely worried about the person I was becoming. When I returned home that night, my family was in shock because they had never seen someone they knew in handcuffs. Only the extreme events like this would cause me to slow down from acting so recklessly and rashly.

Here I was, tearfully reflecting on my past and wondering why God chose to have mercy on such a "bad" person like me. I wondered why God would ever show love or compassion toward someone who had caused so much pain most of her life. Yet, God did.

"...I will have mercy on whomever I will have mercy, and I will have compassion on whomever I will have compassion."

– Romans 9:15

That's when I learned about God's grace and mercy. God is a merciful Father. He is love, and His mercy is why He sent His only begotten Son, Jesus, so that whoever believes in Him shall not perish but have eternal life. God had already paid the price for all of the sins I had committed in my life when He sent Jesus to die for me. How badly I had messed up in life did not matter to God. By leading me to the Cross, I realized that God simply had mercy on me. Nothing I had done or could ever do would deserve the grace and mercy of God upon my life. Coming to that realization completely transformed my heart. God was there throughout all of those episodes in my life, and He saw all of the pain I had afflicted on myself and others. Yet, He still loved me. The powerful act of love and mercy God showed toward me compelled me to forgive others.

Stories of Forgiveness

"For all have sinned and fall short of the glory of God."

– Romans 3:23

I grew up harboring a considerable amount of bitterness toward people, especially my parents. I was born and reared in France. When I was a young child, my father relocated to Cameroon, the home country of both of my parents, for work purposes. As a result, most of my childhood memories do not include him. Later on, during my teen years, my parents separated and eventually divorced.

I never felt stable in my home. I always felt like something was missing, so I spent most of my life searching outside of my home for love and acknowledgment. As a result, I would search for love in friends, in boyfriends, and in other people. When I felt they did not meet my standard for love, I would become bitter toward them. I had a huge void in my heart, and I was desperate for a love that only God could fill. I was trusting in men for my internal strength when only God could fill this gap and strengthen me.

No human being is perfect. Jesus was the only perfect man who ever walked this earth. For any person or even myself to give the kind of love that only God can give is impossible. People had hurt me and I had hurt others, but I now understood that the hurting was the result of our all being broken people. Hurting people hurt people. Everyone has a painful past. Everyone is in need of healing.

God started His first healing work in my life by leading me to forgive others and to acknowledge my wrongs. God was beginning to teach me how to see others the way He sees them. He wanted me to extend mercy to others in the same way He had extended His mercy to me.

One of the most quintessential moments in my life took place during a post-salvation conversation I had with my mom. The last time I had seen her in person was when I was back home in France. During that time, I was still an *unbeliever* (non-Christian). We had a terrible argument, and I blamed her for everything bad that had ever taken place in my life. When I left France, I left her on really bad terms and did not even say goodbye. After departing from France, I did stay in contact with her via phone, but our relationship remained civil at best. However, I was now a new creature in Christ.

One day she called me, and she shared some of the personal issues she was experiencing. In fact, she was going through a difficult time, and she confessed that she did not feel like she had been a good mother to my siblings or me. As she shared her heart, a deep feeling surged in me, and I knew part of her pain came from the years she felt criticized. I knew some of the pain she felt came directly from the years I had spent judging and insulting her.

As she shared her struggles with me, I started crying. The Holy Spirit convicted me, and I knew I had to apologize to her and seek her forgiveness. I told my mom how sorry I was for all of the years I had caused her pain and had insulted her. That moment in my life was eye-opening and completely changed our relationship.

That was also the day I realized I had truly changed. Indeed, I had become a new creature in Christ. I had said "Sorry" to people in the past, but this apology came from a transformed heart.

From that point on, I started forgiving people and contacting those I had hurt to seek their forgiveness. I realized that the more I forgave others, the better I felt. I started comprehending that holding on to grudges and failing to forgive others only imprisons us.

For a great part of my life, I did not understand my dad. I did not live with him for long while growing up as my parents separated when I was young. Although, my dad had remained a part of our lives, it was never enough for me. I always felt that I had no father, and as a result, I developed much resentment toward him. However, after being born-again, God made me realize that my dad did the best he could to rear me. He was not perfect—like I was not perfect. He also needed healing from his past like I needed healing from mine.

God wanted me to see my father and others I had failed to forgive in the same way as He saw them. I had a perfect image of a father in my mind, but only God could truly meet the expectation of perfection. As I have already mentioned, no human being is perfect. My dad had made mistakes like we all have made mistakes in life. Realizing that fact brought healing to my heart.

Overcoming my failure to forgive was indeed a powerful lesson God taught me as a young believer. Before giving my life to Christ, I struggled greatly with my lack of forgiveness. I can recall times when I would become very angry with my younger sister, and as a result, I would spend months without talking to her. I would spend hours analyzing why she was wrong and why I was right. Those moments would cause me to become very sad. Yet, the day God led me to tell my sister that I was sorry for all I had done to her was like a miracle took place. She felt at peace, and I did too.

The great thing about being a Christian is that I no longer had to feel condemned for my past mistakes. For many years, I was embarrassed because I knew it was wrong to insult others, especially my parents. My own sins as an unbeliever condemned me. However, as a Christian, I no longer had to look back at my past and feel ashamed. As long as I confessed my sins to God and turned away from them, God would forgive and redeem me.

On that signature day while I was on the phone with my mother, God completely redeemed our relationship; she forgave me. My relationship with my mother was completely transformed because of what God did during that phone call.

"So now there is no condemnation for those who belong to Christ Jesus." – Romans 8:1, NLT

When we realize our wrongs and forgive others, we are releasing ourselves from the prison of judgment and condemnation. God was showing me that forgiveness truly glorifies Him, and that is how others will truly know that we are His children. Just like God had forgiven me, I felt compelled to forgive others. Learning to forgive was one of the most impactful miracles God performed in my life. As I was growing in my walk with Christ, God was now continuously leading me to seek peace with all men.

"So if you are presenting a sacrifice at the altar in the Temple and

you suddenly remember that someone has something against you,

leave your sacrifice there at the altar. Go and be reconciled to that

person. Then come and offer your sacrifice to God."

– Matthew 5:23, 24, NLT

As a Christian, I was now beginning to understand that my obedience before God had to be complete. I had to come before God in prayer with a clean heart—not a heart full of unforgiveness and strife. The second greatest commandment Jesus left us with was to love our neighbor as ourselves. "Our neighbor" sometimes includes people who have hurt us and even persecuted us. Nonetheless, God expects us to pray for them and bless them (Matthew 5:44). God is the only Judge, and He, Himself, will defend and avenge us.

God Loves You

"Sonya Rolande, who are you? Sometimes I ask myself who I am as
I live in my thoughts and my dreams. My life has not always been
nice. While growing up, I suffered and developed a lot of resentment
toward certain people. For example, my dad, who was absent in my
life, didn't give me too much attention. Because of that lack of

attention, I grew up always looking for love and attention from other people. Most of the time, this quest has been destructive, and I am suffering from my search. I often asked myself about God's existence. Why was He not there when I was suffering? This is a mystery, but I have to learn to move on. Today, I am 22 years old, and I feel like I am 40 or more. I am still looking for myself...who is SR (Sonya Rolande)? A mystery... I still didn't accept myself for who I am. I have a hard time living in my skin, feeling broken by the difference with others. I am black, fat, tall, mean, smart, passionate, ambitious, socially engaged, and depressive at times..."

———

I wrote this note to myself when I was twenty-two years old. I was depressed, and I had a huge identity issue. I gave my life to Christ a year and a half after writing this note. If not for the mercy of God, I believe I could have committed suicide. God saved me just in time.

God is an intentional God! You may be reading this book and feel that my story could also be your story. The truth is that God loves you so much to the point where He sent, Jesus, His only Son to die for you. The issue I had, as a twenty-two-year-old writing this note, was that I was looking for deep love and healing from people, when only God could heal me. God says in His Word that He will never leave us nor forsake us. So all these thoughts I had that He was not there were not true. God was there all along, making a way for me to come to Jesus. God loves us! In fact, looking at my notes, if God did not rescue me on time, I may not be alive today to share my story. But God is a faithful Father. He placed the right people in my life to guide me at the right time.

God loves you too! God made a way to reconcile you back to Him so that you could live life more abundantly—despite your imperfections and your pain. How bad your life has been so far or how badly you think you have messed up in life truly does not matter. Jesus has already paid the price on the Cross to redeem you from all of your sins. Jesus will give you a completely new life in Him—if you will let Him into your heart. Jesus is the truth, the way, and the life (John 14:6). He is the only way for you to have eternal life. All you have to do is to accept Him, which is the easiest and best gift one could ever receive. This gift not only includes a journey of transformation on earth, in which you become born again, but also eternal life in God's kingdom.

Jesus replied, "I tell you the truth, unless you are born again, you cannot see the Kingdom of God." – John 3:3, NLT

Perhaps you are wondering (like I used to), *Where is God?*

Why am I so unhappy and suffering? Know that God is here, and He loves you! He has made a way for you to reconcile with Him. God has promised that He will never leave you nor forsake you. He is waiting at the door of your heart with open arms. All you have to do is let Him in. If you have never made Jesus the Lord of your life, I encourage you to say this simple prayer, out loud, TODAY:

"Jesus Christ, I accept You as my Lord and Savior. Please forgive all of my sins, come into my heart now, and wash me with Your precious blood. Rebuild me from the foundations and lead me to everlasting life in You. In Jesus' name. Amen!" (Romans 10:9)

If you have prayed this prayer, welcome to the family of God! Angels are rejoicing over your salvation (Luke 15:10)! I encourage you to pray that God will lead you to a Bible-believing church where you can study the Word of God and fellowship with other Christians. You can also reach out to me so that I can pray along with you[3]. From now on, start developing your relationship with God by praying and reading the Bible daily (Matthew 6:9-13). Congratulations on making Jesus the Lord of your life!

CHAPTER TWO
Discovering My Identity in Christ

*"Therefore, if anyone is in Christ, he is a new creation; old things
have passed away; behold, all things have become new."*
– 2 Corinthians 5:17

I carried many insecurities coming into the body of
Christ (the church). While growing up, I was always
searching for an identity because I did not truly know who I
was. This struggle continued for me as I entered my teenage
years. I was unable to accept myself for who I was and often
felt rejected by others. Though I grew up in France, my
parents were from Cameroon, and I never felt like I could
fully identify with either of the two cultures. In one, I was
born an immigrant, and in the other, I was a foreign child. I

grew up unsure of my true identity and, as a result, I allowed my environment and others to define who I was. This internal struggle eventually grew to become an external one.

As a teenager, I started rejecting the way I looked and sought for many ways to create an identity. This battle to create my identity led me to start wearing *wigs*. Many women with Afro-textured hair, like myself, wear hair extensions to protect their hair from breakage and for styling. However, I started wearing wigs for the wrong reasons. In fact, I became so insecure with myself that I could no longer display my own natural hair. I wanted to look like people whom I was made to believe were more beautiful than me. For me, wearing a wig gave me an identity and made me more confident in myself.

The truth is that wearing wigs became a bondage—slavery. I was a slave to the wigs I owned. The wigs I wore embodied the internal struggle I faced most of my life. I became bound to wearing wigs for years and refused to uncover my real hair. That bondage eventually followed me, even after giving my life to Christ. However, God was ready to set me free. Before giving my life to Jesus, I was a slave to the world and to the principles of society. As a new creature in Christ, I carried a new identity. God sent Jesus to buy my freedom from everything that held me in bondage. I was no longer a slave, but God's own child (Galatians 4:1-7). I no longer had to remain in bondage to anything. Christ had totally set me free, and accepting His freedom was completely up to me.

"Rise from the dust, O Jerusalem. Sit in a place of honor. Remove the chains of slavery from your neck, O captive daughter of Zion."

– Isaiah 52:2, NLT

I will never forget the day God intervened to deliver me from wearing wigs. That morning, I had joined my church's morning prayer call. One of the prayer points raised was that God would deliver us from bondages. I prayed with all passion on that call, and I was ready to head out to start my day. Of course, I wore my wig as I usually did and was ready to get out of my house.

As I glanced at myself in the mirror to make sure I was ready to go, I felt the Holy Spirit's gently telling me to remove the wig from my head. At first, I resisted the Holy Spirit and pretended that I did not hear Him. Nevertheless, the conviction was so clear that I could not fight it. What had happened was that God was answering my prayers from the morning prayer call. He made the grace available for me to let go of my wig and appreciate my real hair (2 Corinthians 12:9).

I never thought God would pay attention to such a petty area of my life, but He did. God cares about every aspect of our lives. Freedom came to my house that day, and God was about to set me free from years of bondage to wearing wigs. The wig I was wearing on my head that day was the only one I had, and I knew if I threw it away, there would be no turning back. So that was it. My real hair, or should I say the "real me," would be out for the world to see.

I yielded to the Holy Spirit and threw away my wig. Symbolically, by removing my wig, God was truly delivering me from years of personal insecurities and identity issues. The journey to discovering my new identity in Christ and accepting myself began.

"Father, reveal to me every known or unknown bondage in my life and set me free from them, in Jesus' name." (John 8:36)

Christ in Me

"...Christ in you, the hope of glory." – Colossians 1:27

For years, I searched for ways to build an identity without ever being able to find one. I grew up in a society where many people defined themselves by their outward appearance. Trying to discover who I truly was became a lifelong struggle. I never felt at peace within myself because I had allowed the world to define me. The truth of the matter is that there was no way for me to find peace or an identity, unless I surrendered to God. After giving my life to Christ, an immense transformation took place in my life. I was reborn spiritually.

The Bible states that we have a body, a soul, and a spirit (1 Thessalonians 5:23). When we give our life to Christ, our spirit man is transformed and revived. In fact, before Jesus left His ministry on earth to return to heaven, He promised to send His Holy Spirit to His followers (John 14:16). As a new creature in Christ, the Holy Spirit, the Spirit of Christ, was now living in me, and He gave me a spiritual life. The Holy Spirit was now teaching, helping, and guiding me to become all that God had created me to be. I no longer had to chase after an identity and look for people or things to define me. I no longer had to look for others or for my society to approve me. Through Christ, God had reconciled me back to Him. I was finally reconciled back to my Maker—the only One who could tell me who I was since He had made me. He alone could reveal to me my true identity.

"Charm is deceptive, and beauty does not last; but a woman who fears the LORD will be greatly praised." - Proverbs 31:30, NLT

God started teaching me that true beauty had nothing to do with outward appearance but with character. The godly and highly respected woman described in Proverbs 31 was a woman of strong character, great wisdom, many skills, and great compassion. Her physical appearance was never mentioned in the Bible, and her "beauty" came entirely from her character.

In Him, God wanted me to develop the character of Christ not of the world. He needed to remove every bondage the world had placed on my life so that I would be able to realize that I was truly complete in Him. I did not need anyone or anything else to complete me other than Him. Christ in me was all I needed. God wanted me to seek to be like Christ and no longer like the world. My true identity was in Christ. All I had to do was to go back to His Manual for my life, which is the Bible, to discover my identity.

"Father, give me the spiritual wisdom and revelation to grow in the knowledge of who You are and who I am in You. Flood my heart with light so that I will be confident in my identity in Christ Jesus." (Ephesians 1:17, 18)

From spending time in the Bible, I discovered that I was a special gift from God. I was His rich and glorious inheritance. I was not a mistake; I was born for a purpose. God had a calling upon my life, and He had chosen me to join the royal family of Christ. I was now a king and a priest unto Christ and His Father. The Bible was all I needed to know who I was. My identity was found in His Word. Through the Bible,

I could gain knowledge of who God was and who I was in Him.

I must confess that for me to grow in the knowledge of God and who I truly was took some time. As a young Christian believer, I had a lot of passion but not a lot of knowledge and understanding of God's Word. In fact, I rarely spent time reading the Bible, and I was still very insecure as to who I truly was. When I did get around to read the Bible, I lacked understanding concerning what I was reading. Most times, I read the Word of God verbatim, without seeking for a deeper understanding when I did not understand a Scripture. To my great surprise, this lack of the proper interpretation of the Bible led me into a life of bondage all over again…and it all started with a Scripture.

Lack of Understanding

"But a woman dishonors her head if she prays or prophesies without a covering on her head, for this is the same as shaving her head."

– 1 Corinthians 11:5, NLT

When I first read 1 Corinthians 11:5, I was still fairly young in my walk with Christ. I was ready to follow everything according to the Book—no matter if it made sense to me or not. My family had been brought up as Jehovah's Witnesses, which was the only organized religion I truly knew while growing up. In this religion, I had learned not to question what I had been taught for fear of being rebellious. As a result, my view of religion was that whatever you read, you did. I did not know the importance of understanding the context in which Scriptures were written and their purpose in order not to misinterpret them.

I took 1 Corinthians 11:5 literally, and I started wearing a hat to cover my head to church. This misunderstanding grew into real confusion as I became bound to my hat—just like my wigs. I wore a hat on my head at all times. I had made myself believe that since the Bible encourages us to pray all of the time (Ephesians 6:18), I needed to make sure I wore my hat all of the time so that I would always be ready to pray. As a result, I began wearing the hat everywhere.

Little by little, instead of developing a relationship with God, I become religious—very religious. I strictly followed a set of rules, and nothing and no one could stop me. Jesus had set me free, but I still managed to force myself into bondage all over again. Things became worse. Shortly after I began covering my head all of the time, I stopped wearing makeup and jewelry. I also started wearing loose-fitting clothing to make sure my physique was not at all visible through my clothing. I wanted to look as "Christian" as possible.

Somehow, I made Christianity all about the outward appearance. I had become completely religious, but I was yet to learn that Christianity had nothing to do with religion and everything to do with a relationship with God. As funny as it may sound, this season of ignorance lasted for a couple of months but I was convinced that I was doing what God wanted me to do.

"Christ has freed us so that we may enjoy the benefits of freedom. Therefore, be firm [in this freedom], and don't become slaves again."

– Galatians 5:1, GW

For my friends, my family, and pastors to realize that something was wrong with me did not take long. Thankfully, God was very compassionate toward me, and He made sure I did not condemn myself or feel condemned by others. One night, I went to dinner with a close Christian friend who knew something had gone awry with my beliefs.

I had worn a huge t-shirt and a huge skirt. I had a hideous scarf tied to my head. During our dinner, she lovingly asked, "You don't wear earrings anymore?" I know God was actually speaking through her because not long after, another close friend asked me the exact same question. God knew this simple question would not hurt my feelings and would be received in love.

At the time, I was stubborn and convinced that what I was doing was right. I refused to believe God had sent my friends to rescue me. On the outside, I was trying to look confident with my new appearance, but I was not. I was confused about the entire transformation I had inflicted on myself. I was very unhappy doing what I was doing, but I thought I was doing what God was requiring of me. Not until God used my pastor, my mother, and a close mentor to intervene was I able to get true understanding and break free from this new bondage.

"The beginning of wisdom is this: Get wisdom. Though it cost all you have, get understanding." – Proverbs 4:7, NIV

I was about to learn the hard way that reading the Bible required understanding. What had caused months of personal afflictions and insecurities could have been prevented if I had only allowed God to illuminate His Word for me.

Many biblical commentaries are available to provide context to the Holy Scriptures. In 1 Corinthians 11, Paul addresses questions posed by the church in Corinth about women's covering their head during church services. The issue of covering the head had become a big problem in the church because two cultures were in disagreement. A Jewish woman in the church always covered her head during the service, but a Greek woman was used to worshipping God without covering her head. However, at the time, for a woman to uncover her head in public was a sign of immorality. In order to foster church unity and stop the division over the issue of head covering, Paul proposed a solution. Paul instructed the women not wearing a covering to wear one—not because God had commanded it, but to keep the church from arguing over petty issues that would take the minds of the people off Christ.

Some churches today still require women to cover their heads during services. If that is the culture of the church, then it should be respected for the sake of peace. Nevertheless, I was not under any obligation in my church to cover my head. I had heard the story of a woman of God whom God instructed not to wear jewelry. God had done so because jewelry had been an idol in her life. In fact, we have to be very careful not to idolize things because God is a jealous God (Exodus 34:14), and He does not want anything to take His place in our hearts. Nonetheless, God never asked me to stop wearing makeup or jewelry. I had placed these rules on my life—not God.

This painful experience was critical in my journey of learning who God truly is. God desires to have a relationship with us—not a religion. God wants to transform our hearts to become more like His, and He is not as focused on how we look. He wants us to come to Him as we are, and He will never reject us because of our appearance. God wants to develop a *meaningful* relationship with us—not a *meaningless* religion. God is our Father, but He also wants to be our friend.

I still recall the day I realized that I was completely wrong about my crazy transformation. I felt so much freedom. Coming to Jesus brings life and freedom. God is gentle, and we can find rest in Him. Our faith in Christ is easy to bear, not burdensome (Matthew 11:30). After that experience, I felt a little embarrassed over what I had done, and looking at people was not easy. However, God told me not to condemn myself, and that this story was in the past. Most people did not make fun of me; instead, they rejoiced that God had finally delivered me from this confusion and bondage.

Looking back, I laugh about this experience. We do not have to condemn ourselves for the times we fall or make mistakes in our walk with Christ. There is no condemnation in Christ (Romans 8:1); all we have to do is to surrender to God when He corrects us.

I struggled much with condemnation when I first gave my life to Christ. I thank God that as I started learning more about His mercy and forgiving nature, condemnation disappeared. The Bible states in Psalm 103:12 that God has "removed our sins from us as far as the east is from the west." The fact that the east and the west can never meet represents God's forgiving nature. When He forgives our sins, He removes them from us and does not remember them. God forgives and forgets, which is why we should never dwell in the forgiven past and on what we did wrong. God has wiped our record clean. Just like God forgives us, we must also forgive ourselves. We must reject feelings of condemnation and accept His forgiveness and love.

Daily Identity Confessions

I, [your full name], *arise and shine, for my light has come and the glory of the Lord is risen upon me. I put off the old self and wipe away every garment of shame, reproach, condemnation, heaviness, sorrow, [mention others] with the blood of Jesus. I put on the new self, created in the likeness of God in true righteousness and holiness. I wrap myself in the light of the glory of God and clothe myself with the garment of praise, splendor, majesty, strength, power, honor, dominion, favor [mention others]. Indeed, I am fearfully and wonderfully made, in Jesus' name! (Ephesians 4:22–24; Psalm 139:14)*

I decree that I am a new creature in Christ. I am forgiven, justified, sanctified, and holy in Christ. I am complete in Christ. I am God's masterpiece in Christ. I am peculiar, chosen, and called by God in Christ. I am a joint heir with Christ. I am seated in heavenly places with Christ. I reign and have dominion as a royal king and priest in Christ. I am blessed with all spiritual blessings in heavenly places and I am a blessing to my generation in Christ. I am highly favored of God and men in Christ. I have the mind of Christ, and I can do all things through Christ who strengthens me! (2 Corinthians 5:17)

I now decree that the Spirit of the LORD is upon me: the spirit of wisdom, understanding, counsel, might, knowledge, and the fear of the LORD. Therefore, I bear daily all the fruit of the Spirit—love, joy, peace, longsuffering, kindness, goodness, faithfulness, gentleness, and self-control. I do not have the spirit of fear but of power, love, and of a sound-mind. I know who I am in Christ. I am bold as a lion. I silence and condemn every tongue that has or will rise against me in judgment, in Jesus' name! Amen! (Isaiah 11:2; Galatians 5:22; Isaiah 54:17)

CHAPTER THREE
Uncovering the Pain Within

"A woman in the crowd had suffered for twelve years with constant bleeding... She had heard about Jesus, so she came up behind him through the crowd and touched his robe... Immediately the bleeding stopped, and she could feel in her body that she had been healed of her terrible condition." – Mark 5:25–29, NLT

$\mathcal{T}$he woman with the issue of blood described in Mark 5 had gone through a major trauma in her life, before her encounter with Jesus. For twelve years, she endured constant bleeding and no doctor could find a cure to her problem. Her situation had weakened her, and most likely made it impossible for her to live a stable life. The Bible does not describe what was the source of her bleeding. However, we can logically assume that something serious and traumatic must have ignited the bleeding. The Bible confirms that only

Jesus had an answer to her problem. In fact, Jesus knew the cause of her condition, which is why He was able to heal her. Nothing is hidden before God. He knows the source of all pain.

As I began to grow in my relationship with the Lord, God started to uncover a lot of my inner pain. He did not simply bring my past to surface, but He made me understand some of the major sources of my insecurities, fears, and past rebellion. Unknown to me at the time, just like the woman with the issue of blood, I was also bleeding.

I grew up with a lot of anger inside of me. When I was not yelling at my parents or siblings, I was frustrated with myself. Rebelling against my parents, society, and God gave me a false sense of inner peace. It was almost as if I needed to prove to myself and others that I was in control and not weak. It never occurred to me to ask myself why this rebellion started, what ignited these outbursts of anger. Engaging in sexual sins also gave me a false sense of satisfaction as I felt in control of my body and my decisions. Over the years, I started hating who I had become and I no longer took pleasure in being angry or sinning against my body.

When I became a Christian, I found true peace and satisfaction in the Lord. The sins of my past no longer interested me. I had no reasons to go back to them because I had found a God who truly completed me. When I was bored, I knew I could talk to the Lord and rest in His embrace. There was no longer a need for me to be 'entertained' by pornography or other means of self-destruction. Yet, my past was still chasing after me. It was like a chapter of my life would not close until I faced it face-to-face.

I did not know that the Lord was stirring up an urge within me to reconcile with my past in order to truly experience freedom in Christ. Nevertheless, I did not want to revisit parts of my past that seemed shameful or painful. I wanted to move on, forgive and forget. It seems easier to put bandages on a wound and hope it heals than to go through a surgery. However, a wound that is only partially healed will never bring complete restoration.

God is the master surgeon at healing the wounds of our lives. He goes to the deep and inner places that are extremely painful to shed His light. Jesus told us in John 10:10 that he came so that we may have life to the full. I thought that I had forgiven the people who had hurt me, including myself, but God knew that I was like an onion that still needed to be peeled. The truth is that during our time on earth, God will continuously peel us until we meet Him in heaven. Even though my salvation made me feel complete and restored, I was still a *vessel-in-progress*.

God was interested in the why. Why did I grow up with deep anger toward my parents? Why did I feel I abandoned by them and Him? Why would a young child find sexual sins interesting? What originally ignited the bleeding? The answers to each of these questions were very clear to God but too painful for my soul to bear. I did not want to come face to face with myself. It was almost as if I wanted only partial healing. I felt good enough as a new born-again Christian and that feeling was sufficient for me. It was a struggle to let God perform His surgery in my inner being. Yet, God sees everything. God, our loving Father, cannot see us bleeding and not intervene. His nature is to heal, deliver, restore, and not cover up.

Traumas that may have occurred in our childhood or in the course of our lives, such as physical or sexual abuse, can unknowingly cause us to dissociate with ourselves. Dissociation can cause us to disconnect with our feelings, memories, and actions. It is a protective measure used to cope with the intense stress caused by a trauma. The goal of dissociation is to forget the pain caused and numb ourselves from it as much as we can. Dissociation does not erase the impact and consequences of past traumas, it simply shove it under the rug. I dissociated myself with parts of my past unknowingly, which is why I was uncomfortable to allow God to take me through *house cleaning*. But my time for inner healing had arrived.

Inner Healing

God used a dear mentor to make me discover the process of *inner healing* through "Restoring the Foundations Ministry"[4], founded by Chester and Betsy Kylstra. Inner healing is the process God takes us through to heal our soul from past emotional hurts. Through inner healing, we invite the Holy Spirit to reveal to us the true source of our problems, and then we invite Jesus to heal us at the source.

We have to be prepared to receive the truth, which is not always easy to digest. In fact, when the Holy Spirit brings our past to surface, He may rehash memories that we tried for years to erase. At times, the process can seem painful as God takes us back to the event that started the bleeding in our life, but God is there with us to walk us through the process. God may show us things we had no idea about, like He showed me many times.

Inner healing does not entail that God wants us to rehash on the past but that He wants us to find closure. Finding closure implies accepting what has happened in the past and finding healthy ways to transition to the future. Living in denial or dissociating ourselves from reality prevents us from moving forward. In fact, according to the International Society for the Study of Trauma and Dissociation[5], dissociation negatively changes the way a person experiences living. God came to give us an abundant life, not a dissociated one. We have to allow Him into the broken areas of our lives so that He could begin to show us how to live our lives on earth to the full.

One of the most eye-opening and painful wound the Holy Spirit brought to surface was a traumatic incident that happened to me as a very young child. Because I was still very young, I almost completely blocked the incident from my memory. In fact, I remember only fragmented pieces of that event. I was too young to process what had happened, so I thoroughly suppressed the memory (dissociation). However, through the inner healing process I went through, God uncovered the pain: *I was sexually abused as a young girl.* That was one of the main source why I grew up with a lot of anger toward my parents because, as a little girl, I felt that they did not protect me from those who abused me. This trauma is also what ignited my interest in sexual sins as a child. Engaging in sexual sins was a way to numb myself from my past abuses.

God waited until my heart was ready to face this trauma as an adult, and He took me through both the emotional and spiritual healing. In fact, this deep wound had opened doors to sexual perversion, self-hatred, fear, anger, rejection, shame, rebellion, depression, and more sins in my life. God knew that unless I dealt with my inner pain, I would not be able to walk in complete healing and freedom as Christian.

As part of the inner healing process, it was also crucial that I forgave and released the people who had hurt me. I had to let them go in order to be totally set free. Holding grudges and not forgiving will cause us to live a bitter life instead of a better one. Jesus paid the price for all of our sins on the Cross, including the sins of our abusers. I had to release the people who had hurt me in my past—not just to have peace with them, but to have peace within myself.

I had spent years in the prison of anger, bitterness, and resentment. I knew how burdensome it was and how it prevented me from moving forward in life. I no longer wanted to carry that burden. We live in a broken world, and people hurt us because they are hurt and are in pain. As I was allowing God to help me see people the way He sees them, it became easier to forgive and release others for their wrongs.

The true offender is the devil, and he uses people to attack us. Unfortunately, we sometimes end up victims of other people's pain and trauma. Even Jesus said that there is no way to avoid offense in this world (Luke 17:1). Satan will always try to find ways to use people against us. Nevertheless, we cannot judge these people. God is the only and ultimate Judge. We have to trust that God will turn that painful circumstance around for our good.

Another important lesson I learned was whenever we judge others for their wrongs, we actually end up reaping the consequences of those judgements (Matthew 7:2). Michal, David's first wife, was barren all of her life because she judged her husband David (2 Samuel 6:23). Michal had become a bitter and resentful woman due to the challenges she had encountered in her life from her separation, second marriage, and remarriage. Bitterness destroyed her future and brought about barrenness and stagnation in her life. That is why it is crucial we release others whenever they hurt us. Reading the book *How to Stop the Pain*[6] by James B. Richards was also a great blessing. In this book, the author shows how releasing people from our judgements frees us from pain.

Inner healing is a journey. I did not heal from the trauma of child sexual abuse in an instant. I had to rest in God's embrace and grow in my understanding of who I was in Christ. I could not let this past trauma define me. I had to truly accept and believe the fact that I am not abandoned or a victim but a dearly beloved child of God. And yes, I also cried! I realized that because I had dissociated myself from this trauma, I never mourned over what happened to me. Tears release painful feelings. As I cried to God about my childhood pain, I was able to find closure. I told God out loud how I felt and how broken I was. I also asked God challenging questions: Why did He allow me to go through such trauma? Where was He when it happened? Why did He abandoned me then? In fact, the answers God gave me to these questions transformed and healed my relationship with Him and with others, as He helped me to view the world through His lenses.

God did not cause others to abuse me as a child, sin did. God gave Adam and Eve (the first human beings, our first parents) the free will to choose whether they will obey him or sin by following their lustful desires and the devil. They willingly chose to sin against God and this is how sin entered their lives and passed down to us, their descendants. Abuses and traumas arise when people use their free will to do evil instead of doing good. Even though I have never willingly abuse anyone, I have committed many other sins. In fact, all of us on earth have sinned, no men is perfect but Jesus who came to save us (Romans 3:23). God does not intervene every time we are about to make a bad decision because He did not create us to be robot, but He gave us free will. He wanted us to willingly and not blindly love Him. Even though God often intervenes to prevent evil from occurring in our lives, it is not always the case. In fact, God does not always prevent others from hurting us, the same way He does not always prevent us from hurting others. However, God sent Jesus as the solution to save the world from the negative effects of sin. He knew we could not overcome sin on our own, which is why He sent a Savior. In addition, God comfort us through His Word (Romans 8:28) and affirms that, if we allow Him, He will turn the pain and trauma that occurred in our lives around for our good and for His glory.

God never abandoned me even when I was sexually abused. In fact, He made sure to pave a way in my destiny for me to encounter Jesus so that I would experience true healing and victory. As painful and heartbreaking this trauma was, God used it to help me see others the way He sees them. He helped me understand that we live in a painful world, where many are broken and perpetuate their pain on others. Forgiveness is the solution to the pain in our world, which is why God took the first step by forgiving us for sinning against Him and others.

Martha and Mary, in the Bible, were deeply hurt when their brother Lazarus died (John 11). They loved him dearly and believe that God should have intervened to save their brother, but He did not. When Jesus came to see them, they even told Him that if He had come on time, He could have prayed for their brother's healing. Yet, Jesus came after the fact, when their brother was already dead. When Jesus saw their pain, He cried. Yes, Jesus, who is God in human flesh, cried. I believe God cries every time He sees how sin is destroying the world and our lives. God cries when He sees children being abuse, and people being hurt and killed wrongly. I believe God also cries when he sees people using their free will to cause pain and perpetuate darkness in our world. He knows that we are all broken and in deep need of a Savior. God loves us with an unfailing love and He longs to see us whole. He longs to bring healing to our broken heart. Jesus told us in John 16:33 that *"in the world you will have tribulation; but be of good cheer, I have overcome the world."* Even as Christians, we will continue to experience challenges on earth. But Jesus will come back one day to eradicate evil from the world. Until then, He is giving times and opportunities for people to receive Him in their heart as Lord and Savior. While we wait for His return, God is empowering us through ministries such as Inner Healing to overcome the pain caused by sin. God has a glorious way to turn our pain around for our good. We may not see it while we are in pain, just like Martha and Mary. In fact, these two had no idea that Jesus would resuscitate their brother and turn their morning into joy and laughter, which He did. God always has the final say.

Looking back, I thank God for taking me through this inner healing process and for how He helped me cope with the emotional pain of sexual abuse. We do not have to feel condemned, ashamed, or judge ourselves for what happened in our past. Those traumas are part of our life story, and God will redeem everything for our good and His glory. He always gives us beauty for ashes. God does not force us, but if we will allow Him, like He did with the woman with the issue of blood, He can stop any emotional bleeding in our life.

Prayers for Inner Healing

[Protective Prayers (pray out loud and with authority): By the power and authority in the name of Jesus, I forbid any demonic force from manifesting in my life and in my environment. I bind and silence you, and I nail you to the cross, in Jesus' name. I cover all areas of my life and my surrounding in the blood of Jesus.]

1) Sweet Holy Spirit, I am ready to receive Your truth. Reveal to me the pain of my past You want to heal today. [Seat quietly as the Holy Spirit brings things to your remembrance. I encourage you to go through inner healing with a spiritual counselor] *(John 14:26, James 5:14)*

2) Express your emotions and release your pain to God concerning that memory. Tell Him how the pain made you feel. [This step will help you dig further into the wound and bring more things to the surface.] *(Matthew 11:28)*

3) I forgive and release [mention name(s)] *for* [mention what they did to you]. *I break and cancel every judgment* [mention the judgment(s)] *I have made against them. I cancel all the reaping effects of these judgments, in Jesus' name. (Matthew 6:14,*

Matthew 7:2)

4) Jesus, forgive me for the way I have mishandled my pain. I break and renounce my agreement with all of my false comforters [mention the ones that apply: food, alcohol, drugs, people, sex, etc.], *in Jesus' name (Psalm 4:8) .*

5) Lord Jesus, I invite You into this painful memory; come and heal all of my wounds and make me whole. I receive Your healing. [Do not rush this process but give Jesus time to completely heal you. You may start feeling a great peace all around you.] *(Matthew 9:21)*

6) Thank You, Lord, for healing this painful memory. (Mark 5:29)

Uprooting Ungodly Beliefs

"Don't copy the behavior and customs of this world, but let God transform you into a new person by changing the way you think. Then you will learn to know God's will for you, which is good and pleasing and perfect." – Romans 12:2, NLT

Most ungodly beliefs are created due to past traumas and our environment, which can cause our heart to separate from God and His Word. Chester and Betsy Kylstra define ungodly belief as *"All beliefs, decisions, attitudes, agreements, judgments, expectations, vows, and oaths that do not agree with*

God (His Word, His nature, His character)". Many of the ungodly beliefs I had formed came directly from past emotional hurts. I realized later in my walk with the Lord that I had believed the lie that "all men are abusive and perverted" because I was sexually abused by men as a child. I grew up with no real respect for men due to this ungodly belief. In fact, until I became a Christian, I never had a healthy relationship with men. God had to uncover this major lie in my life for me to release men from this judgement I formed against them.

I also formed a major ungodly belief in my childhood, which brought tremendous insecurity in my life. After God finally delivered me from hiding my real hair, I was still very insecure about myself and the way I looked. I simply did not think that I was naturally beautiful, which explained why I spent years without ever revealing my real hair. My thoughts were in direct contradiction with God's Word that clearly states in Psalm 139:14 that we are "fearfully and wonderfully made." I had formed many ungodly beliefs in my mind. God made me realized that being bullied as a child was one of the reasons I struggled with my identity.

I still recall many instances as a child when other children mocked and bullied me for the way I looked. To them, a person of my skin color and features was not beautiful. They were only children, but they had believed and embraced the lies their environment had embedded in their minds. On my end, instead of rejecting these insults and lies, I internalized them. For years, I allowed others and my society to dictate my identity, which made me very insecure about myself.

Satan was not only at the origin of all the traumas in my life but he was also trying to use those bad circumstances to pervert my belief system. A battle was brewing amongst my contrasting beliefs. The ungodly beliefs that had taken root in my mind decades ago sharply opposed the Word of God. It was the devil's word against God's. Over the years, whether consciously or unconsciously, I started agreeing with the word of the enemy. These ungodly beliefs were working against me, and I needed to completely eradicate their power from my being.

Chester and Betsy Kylstra clearly explains in their book, *Restoring the Foundations*, the negative consequences of ungodly beliefs and the negative power they have over our lives. In fact, in their book, the Kylstras described in great detail how ungodly beliefs are formed in our lives and how we can break free from them. Ungodly beliefs must not only be eradicated but they must be replaced with godly beliefs (Ecclesiastes 3:2).

"For the word of God is alive and powerful. It is sharper than the

sharpest two-edged sword, cutting between soul and spirit, between joint and marrow...." - Hebrews 4:12, NLT

The Word of God, which is alive and powerful, carries so much power that it is able to pierce through the most secret and hidden parts of our lives (Hebrews 4:12). When we speak and confess what the Bible says about us, it automatically destroy the evil seeds the enemy tried to plant in our lives. The Bible is a powerful weapon we must use to cancel the lies of the devil. God wanted me to uproot and replace every ungodly belief with His Word. For every ungodly belief, I had to find a Bible scripture that counteracted it. Doing simple searches over the internet, such as "what does the Bible say about (my identity, God's love for me, etc...)", to find biblical scriptures made this exercise very easy.

I started confessing God's Word over my life to overcome my insecurities. One major ungodly belief God revealed to me that I had accepted was that I was "ugly." So, I started confessing Psalm 139:14 over my life. For thirty days, I confessed out loud that *"I am fearfully and wonderfully made"*. Doing that brought tremendous healing even though it was a gradual process. When I would start to feel insecure about myself or if negative thoughts came my way, I would go back to that scripture and speak it aloud again. If you are struggling with identity issues, I highly encourage you to make the

"Daily Identity Confessions" found in the Prayer Index.

Little by little, my thoughts concerning the way I perceived myself changed. I started seeing myself according to what the Bible stated. I started believing that indeed I was wonderfully made, and God loved me exactly the way I was. My life was no longer dictated by what others thought of me, but what I believe God said about me. In fact, I started to believe His Word, which indeed became as powerful as a two-edged sword and destroyed the ungodly beliefs that were planted in me.

Prayers to Break Ungodly Beliefs

1) *Holy Spirit, reveal to me the ungodly beliefs I have accepted in my life, either knowingly or unknowingly* [Take time to make a list of all the ungodly beliefs you can remember and the ones the Holy Spirit reveals to you.] *(John 14:26)*

2) *Father, forgive me for agreeing with the ungodly beliefs that* [mention the ungodly beliefs one by one]. *(1 John 1:9)*

3) *I forgive and release everyone* [mention name(s)] *who influenced me to accept these ungodly beliefs. I also forgive and release myself for believing these lies. (Matthew 6:14)*

4) *I renounce, break, and cancel my agreement with these ungodly beliefs. I cancel all their reaping effects over my life, in*

Jesus' name. (Colossians 2:14)

5) *I accept, receive, and agree with the godly beliefs that...* [Make a sentence and find a scripture that counteract each of the ungodly beliefs. For example, "I accept, receive, and agree with the godly belief that I am fearfully and wonderfully made in the image and likeness of God!". Pray and ask the Holy Spirit to help you form godly beliefs.]

PART TWO

A Season of Deliverance

CHAPTER FOUR
Still Bound?

"If the foundations are destroyed, what can the righteous do?"
– Psalm 11:3

---

*W*hen I gave my life to Christ, my transformation was radical. I went from spending my time smoking, drinking excessively, and engaging in sexual immorality to completely disconnecting myself from these old addictions. Indeed, God had saved me from the kingdom of darkness and translated me into His marvelous light. I truly felt like a new creature. One of the major transformations I experienced almost immediately was the absence of that burning desire to engage in the things of old. The evil desires I had to watch pornography or smoke were gone. I felt completely free. I was convinced that all of my past issues had simply disappeared when I confessed Christ as my Lord and Savior. Yet, God still needed to do something with me in order for me to truly experience the freedom I had in Christ. God needed to repair my broken foundations.

Through my past rebellion, I had willingly (and unwillingly) come to agreement with many evil forces such as sexual defilement, pornography, anger, addiction, and depression. The Bible tells us in Ephesians 6:12 that spiritual forces of evil indeed want to influence our decisions, actions, and life. They are looking for ways for us to agree with them. It could be through continuous outburst of anger, where we unknowingly succumb to forces of bitterness, hatred, violence, rage and anger. Or it could be through negative confessions we make about ourselves such as: "I am ugly, I am a failure," where we unknowingly come to an agreement with spirits of insecurity, depression, self-hatred, and more.

Once we have come to agreement with those evil powers, they have a freeway to come back to influence our decisions and actions. In fact, once we have opened a door to them, they will keep on coming until that door is completely closed. Jesus gives us the power to close all doorways we may have opened to the enemy in our life. He has overcome all forces of darkness and has given us the key to our freedom. In Jesus, we have the authority to tell the forces of darkness to lose their grip over our life.

As a new born-again Christian, I needed to close all of the doorways I had opened to evil. At the time of my salvation, my sovereign God broke the desire for me to rebel like I used to but He also gave me the power, through Christ Jesus, to completely break free from the evil chains of my past. I needed to cut ties with that which held me bound. I needed to declare out loud through prayers and confessions that I would not go back to my old sinful ways. I needed to stand strong in the freedom Christ had given me. This is how I was introduced to the process of *deliverance*.

Deliverance is "the process we go through to break the hold the enemy has over our life due to our sins and/or the sins of our ancestors." Through deliverance, God sets us free from evil agreements we made (knowingly or unknowingly) that prevent us to live victorious lives on earth. That is why Jesus told His disciples in Matthew 10:1 that *"He gave them authority to cast out evil spirits and to heal every kind of disease and illness."* Jesus knew that the people His disciples would encounter would need both salvation (accepting Jesus as their Lord and Savior) and deliverance.

I had been called out of darkness, but all of the evil powers that held me bound in the past did not simply disappear at the time of my salvation. They still had rights to come back to influence me because I had previously opened the door to them and had given them those rights. I believe God in His sovereignty removed the desire to watch pornography and smoke from my life at the time of my salvation. Nevertheless, I still needed to stand on His Word to ensure that I did not return to that sinful lifestyle. I needed to declare in Jesus' name, "I will never go back to watching pornography and smoking." I needed to break my agreement with these evil forces in order for them never to manipulate my life again.

In Christ, we have the power to overcome the bondages of our past, but we still have a choice as to whether we want to stay in bondage or live in freedom. That is why we must stand strong and declare to the enemy that we will no longer go back to our "vomit." When Satan and the evil forces he uses to hurt us see that they can no longer influence our decisions and that we have fully made up our mind, they will flee (James 4:7).

When we first give our life to Christ, the Holy Spirit comes to live within us, and our body becomes His temple (1 Corinthians 6:19). The Holy Spirit then progressively reveals to us what areas of our lives need deliverance. We should not reject this process, but one we should wholeheartedly embrace as Christians.

I recall a specific day when I was still an unbeliever and in bondage to watching shows with pornographic content. I did not know much about "evil forces," but I knew I was perpetually being influenced to go back to that sin. On that particular day, I felt like an evil presence was speaking to my mind and encouraging me to go back to those perverted videos. I wanted to say no to pornography because I knew what I was doing was evil, but I felt as if a stronghold had been built within me to tempt me back to that sin. I was usually frustrated with myself because most times I would yield to those evil influences. It was not as if I had no choice to say no to sin, but I felt very led to say yes.

When the serpent, which represents the devil, came in the garden of Eden, he did not have the power to put the fruit of the tree of the knowledge of good or evil in Adam's or Eve's mouth (Genesis 3). However, through his persistent whispers and lies, he was able to influence Eve's decision to sin first and then Adam's. Yet Adam and Eve chose to eat the fruit with their own hands.

We cannot directly blame the devil or his evil forces for our sins. God gave Adam and Eve the free will to sin or not to sin. They used their free will to commit sin—even though they had a choice. In the same token, I had a choice not to turn on the television and yield to the spirit of pornography.

The issue is that even though God gave us free-will and we can choose it to do what is right, the devil knows that he can easily seduce us into doing what is evil.

Through Adam and Eve, our first parents, we have all inherited a sinful nature. We have a tendency to easily succumb to sin through our sinful nature—our flesh. In fact, the temptation gets even worse once we have gotten used to committing a particular sin. When we have already agreed with a particular sin (by committing it), saying no to that sin in the future becomes even more difficult. The influence of that sin becomes ever stronger and stronger as we continue transgressing, which explains why at one point I felt enslaved to the sin of pornography. My agreement with the spirit of pornography had become extremely strong and had formed a stronghold.

God knew that sin would become a real struggle for humanity, which is why He sent Jesus to free us from the power of sin. Jesus came to earth as a man with a perfect nature because He is God (the second Person of the Trinity). As a result, Jesus could never be seduced by the devil and his cohorts or fall under their influence.

Thus, when we yield our lives to Jesus, He gives us the power to say no to the influences of evil and to cut off their powers from our lives (the deliverance process). As a Christian, I no longer wanted evil to whisper to my being so I embraced the process of deliverance to the fullest.

The Bible reveals to us how some men of God missed

major blessings in their lives due to foundational issues, which could have been solved through deliverance. Moses was one of these chosen men. God favored Moses so much that He spoke to Moses face to face, as a man speaks to his friend (Exodus 33:11). Nonetheless, Moses had a major foundational problem—anger. Throughout his walk with God, that spirit of anger manifested when he killed a man in Exodus 2:12, and also at the edge of his breakthrough when he was about to cross over into the Promised Land. In the latter instance, the Lord commanded Moses to gather the Israelites, to speak to the rock before them, and to command the water to issue from the rock. Moses was frustrated with the constant complaining of the Israelites, so instead of speaking to the rock, he angrily struck the rock twice with his staff to bring forth the water. God was very displeased with Moses' outburst of anger and did not allow Moses to enter the Promised Land.

Another man of God with a foundational issue was Samson, who was supposed to be set apart for God. God had planned to use him to free the Israelites from Philistine oppression. Samson had a glorious destiny, but he only fulfilled part of it because of his bondage to the spirit of lust. Samson could not resist lusting over women, which is how Delilah was able to manipulate him. His foundational struggle overshadowed his ability to discern, and his failure to deal with this issue led him to his destruction.

Solomon was also consumed by sexual lust. In fact, that this issue was an inherited sin from both of his parents, who had committed adultery, is very likely. God had specifically chosen Solomon to rebuild His temple. He gave Solomon great wisdom beyond that of any man who ever existed. Solomon had it all, but the spirit of lust destroyed him.

The Lord had commanded the children of Israel not to intermarry with foreign women as their hearts would turn away from God and toward their heathen gods (1 Kings 11). Just as God had warned, Solomon could not resist his lust for these women and fell away from God.

Failure to deal with foundational issues through deliverance can cause great destructions in our life. In fact, the evil forces attached to those foundational problems can remain dormant until we reach a certain peak in our life, career, or ministry, and then begin to manifest (through their negative influence over our life), leading us to fall.

I knew I had to deal with errors in my foundation as I had opened many evil doors in my life. Unless I prayed to break free from these evil forces, they would try to influence my life again. Christ had paid the price for my sins on the Cross, and He had given me the power to overcome sin. As a born-again believer, I was already standing on the side of victory. All I needed to do was to break my agreement with the sins of my past. I needed to let the devil know he no longer had power over me. The following is how my season of deliverance began.

100 Days of Fasting and Prayer

And when He had come into the house, His disciples asked Him privately, "Why could we not cast it out?" So He said to them, "This kind can come out by nothing but prayer and fasting."

– Mark 9:28, 29

Fasting is a spiritual discipline in which a person abstains from some or all kinds of food or drink or a certain activity for a period of time. The Bible mentions that Paul fasted for three days (Acts 9:9), Daniel fasted for 21 days (Daniel 10:2-3) and Jesus fasted for 40 days (Matthew 4:2). Personally, I have times when I simply fast from meat, or sugar, or social media. Fasting to me is a way of telling God, "I love You more than food or anything else, and You are my main source of satisfaction, pleasure, joy, and delight."

Nothing is wrong with food, and fasting is not an explicit requirement in the Bible, but a discipline that is encouraged. In fact, when coupled with prayer, fasting is a great way to subdue fleshly desires and strengthen our spirit to hear more from the Father. God is always speaking to us, but we can get so carried away with the issues of life that we do not hear His voice or instructions. As a result, fasting, coupled with prayer, enables us to dedicate time to converse with God and hear from Him more clearly.

As the Holy Spirit leads us, we should often take time to fast and pray in order to receive more revelations and clear guidance from Him. By combining prayer with fasting, we are able to build up our spirit man and gain more spiritual stamina. Fasting and prayer also build up our faith. That is why Jesus explained to His disciples in Mark 9:29 that they would have more faith to experience miracles if they fasted and prayed.

My season of deliverance began with a 100-day fast that was announced by my pastor. My church is a part of the Redeemed Christian Church of God (RCCG). The general overseer of our denomination, Pastor E.A. Adeboye, declared a non-compulsory, 100-day fast for all members. I was young in my walk with Christ and very excited to start this spiritual journey. I wanted to get closer to God so that I could receive more revelations from Him about His plans from my life.

During this 100-day fast, I ate no food (but drank water) until 6:00 p.m. every day, and I also set time daily to pray concerning multiple areas of my life. I chose to do my fasting this way, but I know other members of my church chose to fast only from certain foods or only in the morning. Fasting is a personal decision we make with God (Matthew 6:16–18) and not a competition.

Until the 100-day fast started, I was both unaware that I needed deliverance as well as what deliverance truly meant. I simply decided to join the fast in faith, believing that God would do great miracles in my life. I did not know that God would use this fast to bring tremendous deliverance to me.

As Jesus explained in Mark 9, the disciples could not heal the boy with a harassing unclean spirit because they lacked the revelation and faith needed to break the power of that unclean spirit. Through fasting and prayer, a believer can hear God's instructions more effectively concerning all areas of life, including deliverance. In fact, God used this 100-day fast not only to reveal to me the cracks in my foundations, but also the instructions on how to repair them.

Through dreams, God opened my spiritual eyes to realize that what had held me bound for years did not simply disappear. These evil powers from my past had rights to manifest again to cause me to fall. Only then did I start to understand that the devil did not want me to know that I needed deliverance.

I had heard about deliverance in church services, but I was always fearful to learn more. That fear came from the enemy, who did not want me to enjoy the freedom I now had in Christ. Yet God knew the time had come for me to know the truth! This season of deliverance was eye-opening, and I was able to receive great revelation from God. Fasting and praying was not always easy, but God supplied the grace.

The Blood of Jesus

"And they overcame him by the blood of the Lamb."

– Revelation 12:11

During my season of deliverance, I learned vital lessons before engaging in prayer. The first lesson was always to cover myself in the blood of Jesus. This does not mean that we use physical blood; rather, I can say out loud and in faith, "I cover myself in the blood of Jesus." In the spiritual realm, this simple prayer carries a wealth of power. In fact, whenever we are praying to break the power of evil forces, we should always cover ourselves in the blood of Jesus. We can also cover our home in the blood of Jesus.

Exodus 12 explains about the Passover and God's instructing the Israelites to cover their doors with the blood of animals as a symbol of protection. In fact, God had planned to strike all of the firstborn of the Egyptians, but anyone who had the blood on his doors would be protected from that plague. In the same token, the blood of Jesus is our protection from evil. The blood of Jesus is the reason why we have victory over Satan and his army. The Bible tells us in Revelation 12:11 that we overcome the devil and his agents by the blood of Jesus shed on the Cross for our sins. The blood of Jesus is a shield and an effective weapon we can use during prayer.

The Anointing Oil

"And you shall take the anointing oil, and anoint the tabernacle and all that is in it; and you shall hallow it and all its utensils, and it shall be holy." – Exodus 40:9

Concerning my home, God has taught me always to anoint and pray over the house into which I move. Anointing oil is often used for protection, and we can apply it to ourselves and our belongings or environment. In the Bible, the anointing oil was used to sanctify things, people, and places (Exodus 40:9); for deliverance when breaking evil strongholds (Mark 6:13); to heal the sick (James 5:14); and also in commissioning a person for service to God (1 Samuel 16:13).

To anoint my home, I simply use an oil, usually olive oil, and pray that God will anoint it with His presence and power. I dab a small amount of anointing oil on any doors or windows or items in the house. I also go from room to room, speaking peace and blessing over each room and commanding any evil presence to vacate my property in Jesus' name (Luke 10:19). Yes, evil forces can reside in someone's home, and I believe God used an interesting experience I had in an apartment I lived to make me realize that possibility.

One time a friend came to visit and stayed with me in my apartment. Every time we were specifically at home, she would constantly argue with me. I did not understand why she was continually attacking me. I noticed that she would get especially argumentative with me in my apartment. She only resorted to that aggressive behavior in my apartment.

One day I felt God telling me to pray over my home and command every evil presence to leave immediately (Matthew 15:13). Right when I was done praying over my home, my friend came back. To my surprise, her behavior dramatically changed, and she was not as aggressive toward me. I also personally felt peace in the apartment. Only then did I realize that an evil force might have been present in my house to bring in division and violence.

When we move into a new home, we are not always knowledgeable about what the people who lived there before us were engaged in. Some people engage in evil and violent activities such as witchcraft or abuse, and thus, allow many forces of darkness to dwell in their homes. If we ever move into such a home, the evil forces that were there will most likely remain unless we kick them out. God taught me to use the power I had in Christ to take authority over the atmosphere of every home into which I move. I highly recommend reading *"Protecting Your Home from Spiritual Darkness"* by Chuck Pierce,[7] which was a great blessing to me and very eye-opening.

Fear Not, You Have Power

"Behold, I give you the authority to trample on serpents and scorpions, and over all the power of the enemy, and nothing shall by any means hurt you." – Luke 10:19

One thing Satan does not want us to know is that we have power as Christians. The enemy wants us to be fearful of him and his evil agents. Nonetheless, the Bible makes it clear that, in Christ, we have power over them. In addition, Jesus told His disciples that the enemy would not be able to hurt them when they prayed (Luke 10:19). In fact, Satan may temporarily try to bring afflictions to our life, but he would never be able to hurt our eternal welfare as long as we have surrendered to Christ.

Whenever we use the power and authority Christ has given us to fight against evil, we must be confident that we are on the winning side. Jesus has already conquered the victory for us. All we are doing is exercising the power Jesus gave us through prayers and claiming our victory. We do not have to fear what the devil will do to us when we pray.

As a young believer, I was terrified of the devil, and for me to understand the power of prayer was very important. I did not yet understand my position in Christ, and I was easily intimidated every time I prayed any serious prayer such as a prayer for deliverance. What God showed me was that I needed to be bold in the place of prayer and not allow any evil force to intimidate me.

Intimidation happens to be one of Satan's favorite tactics. He tries to intimidate us so that we think his power is greater than the power of Christ. However, the Word of God stands sure: *"He who is in you is greater than he who is in the world."* (1 John 4:4). We have absolutely no reason to be afraid when we pray.

Experiencing resistance from evil forces after we pray is possible. In fact, whenever we engage in spiritual warfare, which is taking a stand against evil, the devil will try every strategy to stop us. We do not have to be fearful or discouraged when these times come. All we have to do is to persist in prayer to become bolder and stronger.

When I first started praying for deliverance, the devil started using people to attack me. For no reason, certain people would become angry with me or suddenly become very argumentative. During these times, I needed to make sure that I did not get angry at them, but to understand that the devil was using them in attempts to hinder my prayers.

Satan can even try to use fellow Christians to attack us. If these people are not spiritually discerning, they will not realize that they are being negatively influenced. The devil knows any lack of forgiveness toward another will hinder answers to our prayers (Matthew 5:23). However, we cannot allow him to intimidate us or hinder answers to our prayers.

Whenever we experience resistance after we have prayed, we cannot back down; we have to persevere. In Acts 4:29, the believers prayed for boldness after experiencing persecution. They did not back down. They simply asked God to make them bolder, and He did. For some time, I also added Luke 10:19, 2 Timothy 1:7, Proverbs 28:1, and Philippians 4:13 to my list of daily confessions to help me become stronger and bolder in the place of prayer. I could not allow fear to cripple me and prevent me from enjoying the total freedom Christ had given me. I had to hold on to the fact that I was sitting in the victory seat of Christ, and I could do all things through Christ who was now strengthening me (Philippians 4:13).

"Thank You, Lord, for giving me authority and power over all the powers of the devil! I take authority over every spirit of fear and intimidation, and I forbid your operation in my life, in Jesus' name. I command you to loose your hold over my prayer altar, in Jesus' name. I know who I am in Christ; I am bold as a lion!"

(Luke 10:19, Acts 4:29, Proverbs 28:1)

Warning

"And the evil spirit answered and said, 'Jesus I know, and Paul I know; but who are you?' " – Acts 19:15

The sons of Sceva in Acts 19 were calling upon the name of Jesus without knowing Him personally. They engaged in occult practice for money and were casting demons from witchcraft. They were impressed by Paul, whose power to cast out demons was more powerful than theirs. In fact, Paul's power came from God's Holy Spirit. Yet, the sons of Sceva thought they could duplicate this power by using the name of Jesus to cast out demons.

Their actions backfired on them. The evil spirit did not recognize who they were because they did not have authorization to use the name of Jesus. Only those who have surrendered their lives to Christ have that authorization. So as they tried to cast out the demon from a man by using the name of Jesus, the demon instead came upon them and brutally attacked them. They were left completely bruised and naked.

The Bible tells us in Luke 10:19 that when we pray against evil forces, nothing shall hurt us. However, we must first surrender our life to Jesus and accept Him as our Lord and

Savior before we can use the power in His name. This ensures that when we pray, we do not come back with wounds but victorious. The day we give our life to Jesus, Heaven records our name, and we are given the authorization to use the name of Jesus.

Deliverance Requires Perseverance

"But I will not drive them out in a single year, because the land would become desolate and the wild animals would multiply and threaten you. I will drive them out a little at a time until your population has increased enough to take possession of the land."

– Exodus 23:29, 30, NLT

Deliverance requires a plethora of patience and perseverance. An abundance of care needs to be taken after we are delivered from a particular condition (such as pornography). If we go back to our old ways, the devil can come with seven stronger evil forces to afflict us, and our condition will only worsen (Matthew 12:45). We have to make up our mind that we would not go back to being in bondage, before praying for deliverance. I recall a time after I gave my life to Christ when I almost backslid. I was still "in love" with my former boyfriend, and I almost went back to committing sexual sins with him. God used this episode of my life to teach me the importance of learning how to resist temptation and not allow evil to influence my actions any longer. I had to be willing to change and surrender to the directions of the Holy Spirit. I could not allow the romantic words of my former boyfriend to lure me back into bondage.

Deliverance, like salvation, is a choice. We have to be willing to let our "old nature" die in order to receive Christ's salvation, healing, and deliverance. The devil finds many ways to try to seduce us back into sin, so we have to be spiritually discerning to stand strong in our walk with Christ. For me to find accountability partners and mentors, with whom I could share my struggles and who would pray with me when I felt tempted to sin was so important. Resisting the temptation to sin is a life-long journey, as the devil is relentlessly trying to make us fall. However, God's grace is sufficient to sustain us, even when we fall at times.

Deliverance also requires some mental preparation. We have to be willing to receive the freedom Christ gives us and be teachable. We have to allow God to show us the issues in our foundations and let Him take us through the deliverance process. The person seeking deliverance has to be open and humble to receive the truth, which is not always easy at first. When God first revealed to me that I needed deliverance, I was completely terrified. Yet I yielded to His instructions. I had grown in my walk with God and knew that God wanted only what was best for me. So I needed to trust Him and believe that He was working all things for my good. We are more than conquerors in Christ. We cannot allow Satan to rob us of the blessings of deliverance. Jesus came to set the captives free so that we would never have to be bound again. We must make the decision to receive all of the blessings we have in Christ.

CHAPTER FIVE
Examining My Dreams

"Call to Me, and I will answer you, and show you great and mighty things, which you do not know." – Jeremiah 33:3

---

*G*od can speak to us through dreams (Acts 2:17). *Dreams* are simply "series of images we experience while we sleep." Dreams can be instructions or revelations of activities that occur in the spiritual realm or that will occur in the future. God longs for us to grow in our spiritual walk with Him and discover all that He has purposed for our life. God knows that while we are awake we are sometimes too preoccupied with things and thoughts that we may not discern when He is speaking to us. However, when we are at rest and sleep, He is able to get our attention, which is one of the reasons why we should examine our dreams and pay close attention to them. If you have never dreamed or if you do not remember your dreams, simply ask the Holy Spirit to give you revelations through dreams and to help you to remember them. God does not show favoritism, so He can speak to you through dreams like He did for many others, including me. For those who dream, it is important not to ignore the dreams that we have. We should carefully examine them and even write them down. In fact, some dreams could be revelations from God about our life or that of others.

Through dreams, God can reveal things to us concerning our past, future, or even give us warnings concerning our life. I have experienced tremendous deliverance through the revelations God has given me in my dreams. Through dreams, God took me back to past events that occurred in my life and revealed things about which I had no idea or had completely forgotten.

He showed me areas of my life needing healing that I would have never known if it had not been for His divine revelation. In fact, we often bury and cover wounds too deep and hurtful to address. God shines His light in places in our life that need permanent healing so we can live the abundant life He purposed for us.

God has also used dreams to reveal to me things about my future so that I will make the right decisions when the time comes. God is an encourager, and He has also used dreams to show me some of the amazing things He planned to do in my life. For us to seek God's face and ask Him to give us revelations about our lives is crucial. If He wills, He can choose dreams as a means to do that.

Nevertheless, not every dream comes from God. Some dreams can be formed of our imaginations, and others dreams can be demonic (from evil spirits). We have to ask God for the ability to discern the source of our dreams and rightly examine and interpret them. The Bible tells us in James 1:5 (KJV), *"If any of you lacks wisdom, let him ask of God, who gives to all liberally and without reproach, and it will be given to him."* God gave Daniel the special ability to interpret the meanings of visions and dreams (Daniel 1:17). If we ask God, He can also bless us with the same gift He gave Daniel.

I have learned to always ask God to help me interpret the dreams I have. Usually, if my dreams concerned divine revelations (prophecies) about my future, I check to confirm that they are aligned with the Bible. If that is the case, I write them down and continually pray until these prophecies are fulfilled. If my dreams are strange in nature or seem to be warnings from God, I would ask God for the wisdom to interpret them and then pray accordingly.

Once, I saw myself in an accident in a dream. This dream did not necessarily mean that an accident would occur, but that I needed to beware and pray that it would not take place. My simply taking the dream for granted could have been tragic. God has also led me to share my dreams with my Christian mentors for guidance or for them to pray with me. However, we should exercise discretion concerning with whom we share our dreams and ensure that they have the spiritual wisdom to properly guide us.

In fact, some dreams should be kept secret. In Genesis 37 Joseph's sharing his dreams had tragic results when he excitedly told his brothers how God had showed him in his dreams that he would rule over them. Joseph's brothers did not protect his dreams; rather, they were jealous of the revelations he was receiving from God. Instead, they tried to destroy Joseph so that his dreams will never come to pass. Joseph should not have boasted about his dreams. The correct response to the dreams he was having was to keep them to himself. Thanks to God, Joseph still fulfilled his destiny, but he learned along the way that he had to guard his dreams. God warned me that, like Joseph, I had to be very careful with whom I share my dreams.

Dreams should not be ignored, but examined. We need to guard our dreams and carefully investigate the different activities that are occurring while we are asleep. I encourage you to read James W. and Michal Ann Goll's book, *Dream*

Language,[7] to better understand the power of dreams and how to interpret them.

Repeating Dreams

"It is the glory of God to conceal a matter, but the glory of kings is to search out a matter." – Proverbs 25:2

God has used dreams many times to reveal secrets about my life about which I had no idea or had forgotten. One particular time God repeatedly started revealing something to me in multiple dreams. I felt as if God wanted to get my attention and for me to take a matter seriously.

As a result, I started paying more attention to my dreams, especially if the same dream were reoccurring more than once. God can repeat a prior dream to get our attention on a specific matter so not ignoring our dreams is important. Repeated dreams can imply a warning or a confirmation from God about a situation.

Many times when I missed the interpretation of a dream, God would bring the same dream again so that I could seek counsel or pray further about the meaning of that dream. Yet repeated dreams can also have different meanings. Genesis 41:32 explains that repeated dreams could also mean that *"…these events have been decreed by God, and He will soon make them happen."* In fact, repeated dream could be confirmation that a certain event is bound to happen. We must ask the Holy Spirit for the proper interpretation and response to what we have seen in our dreams.

I recall a time when I was having repeated dreams about someone with whom I had become close. In one dream, God showed me that this person was not a good friend to have in my life as she would influence me to do things that were contrary to His will for me. However, because this person was extremely friendly, I refused to believe that God was right—even though I was fully aware that God knows the heart of all men and women.

After a couple of weeks of being around that person, I started seeing changes in her behavior. I realize that she was not as trustworthy as I thought. Yet still, I was not fully convinced that I should be careful about interacting with her. I did not think that she could cause me to stumble.

So God gave me another dream in which I saw myself doing something bad. In the same dream, I saw that friend coming toward me and encouraging me to continue doing what I was doing. She even insisted in the dream that she would join me in that wrongdoing.

When I woke up, I knew God was right. In fact, I realized that since I had become her close friend, I had started thinking of compromising some of my Christian values. I felt that she was leading me to believe that some of the wild things I had done in my past were acceptable ways of life and that I could continue in these behaviors. God gave me the wisdom through His multiple warnings in my dreams to gently separate myself from her.

God has also used repeated dreams to make me realize areas of my life in which needed deliverance. With those dreams, I often had a harder time interpreting their meaning. Sometimes, God uses symbols, people I know, particular settings in my dreams to illustrate points He is trying to make or a message He is trying to convey to me. I had to learn over the years how to interpret certain dream languages God used with me. Nevertheless, I always pray for understanding as different dreams, even if similar, can have different meanings.

I recall dreams when I saw myself swimming multiple times in the sea as if I were lost and trapped in the sea. I would keep on having the same repeated dreams about swimming in the sea around the same time. I had no idea what these dreams meant, but I knew they had an important meaning since God kept on repeating them.

Finally I reached out to one of my mentors who has been in the ministry of deliverance for decades. She joined me in prayer to figure out the interpretation of these dreams of my swimming in the sea. God revealed to my mentor that I needed to pray against marine spirits. However, swimming in the dream may not necessarily relate to marine spirits, so the person has to ask the Holy Spirit or seek godly counsel for understanding of dreams. In my case, God had been instructing me to pray for deliverance against the influence of marine spirits in my life. I would not have figured out on my own what the dreams meant especially since I had no idea what marine spirits were.

"In that day the LORD will take his terrible, swift sword and punish Leviathan, the swiftly moving serpent, the coiling, writhing serpent.

He will kill the dragon of the sea." – Isaiah 27:1, NLT

The Bible refers to marine spirits such as Leviathan in Isaiah 27:1 and Psalm 74:13, 14. In Arabic, *leviathan* means "the twisted animal," which is regarded in the Bible as a creature of the waters, a sea monster, a sea-serpent, or crocodile. The expression of *leviathan* in the Bible is metaphorical and can be understood as powerful enemies of the people of God.

Pharaoh, the king of Egypt, who oppressed the Israelites, was also described in Ezekiel 32:2 as a monster in the seas. Pharaoh was influenced by the spirit of pride, rebellion, destruction, and death. Revelation 13:1 also refers to "the beast of the sea," which represents kingdoms that will try to exercise great cruelty upon Christians. These kingdoms are dominated by sexual perversion, witchcraft, murder, greed, and more evil. Marine spirits are spiritual forces that try to bring destruction into our lives.

God was using dreams to show me that I needed to break my agreement with these evil forces. As a new creature in Christ, I had made up my mind that I would no longer yield to lust, perversion, pride, rebellion, and destruction (marine spirits). I needed to pray to stop the influence of these evil forces in my life. Jesus had paid the price for all of my sins so they no longer had rights to influence my life. I fasted and prayed for couple days, and the dreams about my swimming in the waters stopped. I knew my agreement with these marine spirits had been completely broken off in my life.

"God, dry up the powers of marine spirits trying to influence my life. I come against the operation of marine spirits in my life, in Jesus' name. Loose your hold upon my life. I break every link with the marine kingdom with the blood of Jesus."

(Jeremiah 51:36, Isaiah 27:1)

Interpreting Deliverance Dreams

From the time my season of deliverance began, God used dreams to show me things about my life about which I had no idea. To my surprise, God also used dreams to bring tremendous deliverance in my life. Through dreams, God started revealing to me the evil spiritual forces that were trying to influence and attack my destiny. He opened my spiritual eyes to understand how the attacks manifesting in the physical realm actually take root in the spiritual realm. The human being is composed of a body, a soul, and a spirit (1 Thessalonians 5:23). The state of our spirit and what happens to it in the spiritual realm is extremely important. God is a Spirit, which is why He communicates with us through His Spirit. The devil and his evil forces are also spirits. They fashioned their attacks against our life in the spiritual realm. For instance, the devil can try to negatively influence people's spirits so that they start manifesting evil behavior in the physical such as bitterness and depression.

Through dreams, I began to understand how important it was for me to stay connected to God's Spirit through praying. I needed to pray more effectively and to carefully examine the ways He would respond back to me such as through dreams.

I recall a time when I was seeing myself back in high school, either inside or around the school. I felt as if I were simply wandering and could not really move to a higher level in life. I was simply stuck around my high school. At the beginning, I thought nothing was wrong in seeing myself back in high school. In fact, I assumed that I was simply recollecting episodes of my past. However, when God started repeating these dreams, I realized they probably had a deeper meaning.

I started praying for the interpretation of these school-related dreams, and I felt the Holy Spirit's telling me to pray against the spirit of backwardness and stagnation. I also prayed with a deliverance minister who felt that God was telling her the same thing. An important point to note is that seeing ourselves in high school or in a school may not be bad. The dream could simply imply that God was taking us through learning process or a season. That is why I want to reiterate the importance of asking the Holy Spirit for the proper interpretation of dreams. In my case, the Holy Spirit revealed to me that I needed to pray against the spirit of backwardness and stagnancy in that season of my life.

The spirit of backwardness causes wasted efforts and constant failure at the edge of breakthrough. Every time the person tries to take a step forward, this spirit pulls him backward. This spirit also relates to the spirit of stagnation. In John 5, we read the story of the sick man who was lying by the pool of Bethesda. Verse 4 relates that, at certain times, an angel of the Lord would go down to the pool and stir up the water. And whoever stepped in the water after it was stirred would immediately recover from his or her infirmity.

This sick man at the pool of Bethesda had been attacked by the forces of backwardness and stagnancy for 38 years. In fact, for 38 years, every time the angel came to stir the water, this sick man tried to be the first to step into the water, but each time someone went ahead of him. As a result, he never had the opportunity to move forward, but he remained stagnant and ill.

Not until he encountered Jesus was he able to gain deliverance from the forces of backwardness and stagnancy. For 38 years, he took steps forward into the pool to gain deliverance from his sickness, but every time he tried, someone rushed in front of him, and he had to go backward again. How disappointing and frustrating that yearly experience must have been. In fact, spirits of backwardness and stagnancy are forces that hold people back and prevent them from reaching higher levels in life.

What surprised me about these particular dreams was that they were occurring in a season of my life when I was struggling financially and could not find a job. I felt as if God was revealing to me the spiritual warfare behind my struggles. These spiritual forces of stagnancy and backwardness were trying to manifest in my life to prevent me from moving ahead financially.

These specific dreams helped me to understand how the spiritual realm can influence the physical realm. As I began to align my prayers based on the deliverance dreams and instructions I was receiving from God, I started seeing a shift in the physical realm. The influences of backwardness and stagnancy were being broken off my life. God was giving me the wisdom to bring the spiritual realm in alignment with His perfect will and purpose for my life.

 "I come against every spirit of backwardness and stagnancy operating in my life, in Jesus' name." (John 5:1–9)

In another type of deliverance dream I saw someone driving me away from the road God wanted me to take in my destiny. I was sitting in the backseat of a car, and the driver took the wrong road. Seeing someone's driving us in our dreams most likely means that the person possesses some sort of positive or negative control over us. If it is negative, we need to pray against the spirit behind it. In fact, it could be the devil's tactic to divert us from the plans God has for our life. The Bible states in Proverbs 14:12 that *"there is a way that seems right to a man, but its end is the way of death."* The entire plan of the enemy is to ensure that we take the path of death and not the path of life, which God has traced for us. I believe that God was warning me in that season of my life to be careful of the advice I was receiving from certain people and of the decisions I was about to make. These dreams helped guide my prayers in order to bring my destiny in proper alignment with God's will.

"I come against every spirit of diversion, in Jesus' name."

Another set of deliverance dreams occurred when I was studying for a professional exam that would have enabled me to grow in my career and be financially stable. In the dream, I saw myself studying for that exam, but I was unable to complete it, which led to my failure. In another dream, I saw myself as being unable to actually get to the exam center so I failed the exam.

While praying, I asked the Holy Spirit for an interpretation of those dreams, and I felt led to pray against the spirit of incompletion and failure. Many times while studying for that exam, I felt as if I was incompetent, and I was fearful that I would fail the exam regardless of how much I studied. God was simply revealing to me the evil forces behind those thoughts. The devil's plan is always to steal, kill, and destroy (John 10:10), which explains why there was a spiritual battle to ensure my failing the exam so I would not progress.

I had to stand strong on God's Word and rebuke those evil forces. I also added biblical confessions on faith to my daily prayers that helped motivate me while I was studying. Now that I was equipped with this spiritual knowledge, I had to guard myself from any influence that would lead me to believe that I would fail my exam.

Nehemiah chapters 4 and 6 tell about the opposition that arose when Nehemiah decided to rebuild the walls of Jerusalem. The spirits of incompletion manifested through Sanballat, Tobiah, and other enemies who tried to stop Nehemiah from completing his divine assignment. He was mocked and threatened by his adversaries, but through prayer, he was able to overcome these attacks. The devil does not want us to complete the plans God has for our lives, but God has already given us victory in Christ Jesus. To the glory of God, I passed my professional exam on the first try with a very high score.

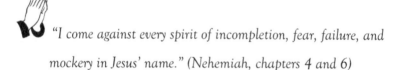 *"I come against every spirit of incompletion, fear, failure, and mockery in Jesus' name." (Nehemiah, chapters 4 and 6)*

At a time when I felt my mind was heavily influenced by the spirit of lust, I recall moments when I would catch myself staring in a perverted way at people. I felt was as if the devil had gained some control of my mind. I was using 2 Corinthians 10:5 to pray against these evil activities in my mind, but they kept returning. I knew something was wrong, so I prayed to God to show me the source of the issue. One day, God revealed the spiritual warfare issue behind this struggle in a dream.

I saw myself leaving an apartment building in Marseille, France, in which I had lived as a child. I also saw an evil man follow me from the building where I once live. Then I saw myself taking a train to Paris, France, to where my family had moved around the time I turned nine. The evil man who had followed me from Marseille was still there with me. Suddenly, this evil man started cursing and lusting over other women who were on the train.

What God was showing me is that the spirits of lust and perversion had followed me from places where I had lived because I had made agreements with them. So after praying and breaking my agreement with these evil forces, to the glory of God, these perverted attacks in my mind finally stopped. The more deliverance dreams I was having, the more I could understand how the spiritual realm influences the physical realm.

"I bind and cast out every evil spirit that has followed me from places I have lived. I disconnect myself from you with the blood of Jesus, and I command you to loose your hold over me, in Jesus' name." (Revelation 12:11)

I also recall deliverance dreams involving smoking. In one dream, I saw myself in a house full of smokers, and everyone looked like addicts. In another dream, I saw myself smoking in the backseat of a car with men sitting by me. I appeared to be somehow trapped like a prisoner. I also saw myself in another dream with people who were smoking around me, and I was being contaminated by the smoke.

I ignored the first two dreams, simply assuming they were dreams about my past life, since I used to be a smoker. I wrongly thought that I had simply dreamed of the things I used to do. However, through prayers and guidance from a deliverance mentor, I realized that my dreams were actually revelations concerning past agreements I had made with spirits of addiction.

In the past, I used to smoke heavily, but the day I gave my life to Jesus, God, in His sovereignty, removed my desire to smoke again. However, I had never broken my agreement with these spirits of addiction. In the spiritual realm, everything is governed by rights or agreements. If you give the right to Jesus to be your personal Lord and Savior, His Spirit will come and dwell in you to help guide you in the right direction. In the same token, if you give rights to the devil and his evil forces through committing sins, they have the right to come back to influence your life negatively. God does not break this principle.

Jesus gives us the power to cancel any right we have given to the enemy, but we ourselves must make those declarations.

God has given us free will to make decisions on our own, and breaking our agreement with the sins of our past is one of the decision we have to make. Jesus gives us the grace to let go of our past sins and addictions as we surrender to His Spirit.

On the day of my salvation, Jesus gave me both the grace and power to let go of smoking. I had to exercise this power I acquired in Christ Jesus to break my agreement with these forces of addictions so that their demonic influence would be completely broken off my life.

Please note that smoking in a dream may not necessarily mean a spiritual attack, but it could be a warning from God that we are engaging or about to engage in something that could be detrimental to our wellbeing. I would not be surprised if there are other meanings to smoking God uses to interpret dreams. That is why it is important to ask the Holy Spirit for the proper interpretation of our dreams.

Prayers to Break Free from Addictions

1) Father, I repent for coming to agreement with the spirits of addictions to smoking tobacco, marijuana, [mention others] in my life. I renounce and break my agreement with these addictions, in Jesus' name. (1 John 1:9)

2) I take authority over the strongman of addiction to smoking tobacco, marijuana [mention others]; *I bind and cast you out of my life, in Jesus' name. I incubate my body, soul, and spirit in the fire of the Holy Spirit. (Luke 10:19, Hebrews 12:29)*

3) I come against every contamination and pollution through the dream, in Jesus' name. (Matthew 13:25)

4) Holy Spirit, fill me up so there would be no room for evil in my life, in Jesus' name. (1 Corinthians 6:19)

5) Holy Spirit, guide me to Holy Spirit-filled men and women of God who will keep me accountable for my actions, like Nathan held David accountable, in Jesus' name. (2 Samuel 12)

5) I come against every resistance to my prayers, in Jesus' name. I cover my body, soul, and spirit in the blood of Jesus. (Revelation 12:7, Revelation 12:11)

[You can also apply some anointing oil on your forehead (see page 73, Isaiah 10:27)].

6) I thank You, Lord, for answered prayers! (Luke 17:15, 16)

Demonic Dreams

"And the LORD said to Satan, "The LORD rebuke you, Satan! The LORD who has chosen Jerusalem rebuke you!"

– Zechariah 3:2

The devil tried to manipulate my dreams on numerous occasions to make me think that particular dreams were from

God when, in fact, they were not. Demonic dreams started in my childhood. I recall as a child when I would have terrible nightmares, which engendered much fear in my being. Until I gave my life to Christ, I could not sleep in a dark room because of my agreement with the spirit of fear, which had started influencing my life from my childhood through demonic dreams.

Demonic dreams can become a source of bondage if they are not dealt with. I believe we have to be very prayerful concerning our dreams to ensure we understand both their sources and meaning. Demonic dreams are usually not aligned with the Bible, and they yield fear, sexual perversion, and confusion. They are usually schemes from the devil to intimidate us.

In one of my demonic dreams, I saw myself masturbating. When I awakened, I knew right away the dream was not a revelation from God, but from the devil to pervert my life and influence me to sin. This demonic dream was also a pitiful strategy of the devil to make me condemn myself because of my past and generate shame. In the dream, I looked like I was in bondage. However, I knew I had broken my agreement with the spirits of sexual perversion. Just like the Lord did in Zechariah 3:2, I had to rebuke Satan and command him to let go of my dream life. In fact, the devil had no rights to influence me concerning sexual sins since I had broken my agreement with him. I had to be confident in my deliverance and not doubt the authority Jesus had given me. I had to stand against the enemy and remind Him of my freedom in Christ.

I also believe in the importance of prayer for divine protection before going to bed (Psalm 91) to avoid those types of demonic dreams. God promised in His Word that He gives His children sweet sleep (Psalm 4:8, Psalm 127:2), so we have to believe His Word and remind the devil of it too!

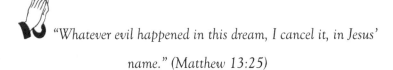 *"I come against every spirit of confusion and manipulation in the dream, in Jesus' name. Satan, I rebuke you. Loose your hold over me and my dream life, in Jesus' name." (Zechariah 3:2)*

As a rule of thumb, whenever we have dreams that seem evil or contrary to the will of God for our lives (Jeremiah 29:11), we should cancel them in prayer. A prayer I usually pray when I wake up and I am aware that I had a bad dream is as follows:

"Whatever evil happened in this dream, I cancel it, in Jesus' name." (Matthew 13:25)

Some demonic dreams can occur when we have not

broken our agreements with certain evil forces. In fact, they can manifest while we are sleeping to scare and intimidate us. I believe God sometimes allow those demonic dreams to force us to seek deliverance. If you are suffering from demonic attacks in your sleep, I highly recommend that you seek help from your church leader(s), who will be best equipped to guide you through your deliverance or connect you with a deliverance ministry. I also encourage you to visit the Ransomed Heart Ministries' online page[12]. The ministry has a "Bedtime Prayer" confession, which I found very effective when I went through a season of persistent attacks in my sleep. It is well; the Lord is with you!

Dream Sanctification

"No weapon formed against you shall prosper, and every tongue which rises against you in judgment you shall condemn."

– Isaiah 54:17

Throughout my season of deliverance, I received many revelations from God through dreams, which is why I was not surprised when the devil started fighting back and attacking my dream life. The enemy did not want me to obtain revelations from God because I was experiencing a great deal of healing and deliverance. So Satan tried to make my sleep a total nightmare.

Evil forces started feeding me and cursing me while I was sleeping. Usually when I see evil forces in the dream, they look like human beings with very evil looks. So I could not really sleep for a full week because every time I would close my eyes, I would see someone evil trying to feed me bad food. In one dream I also heard a voice cursing me and telling me to die. At the beginning, when these dreams started occurring, I had no idea they were demonic. I thought they were caused by my poor eating habits at the time, or that I was likely hungry. I ignored these demonic dreams until I realized that they were now occurring every time I closed my eyes to sleep.

God led me to share these evil dreams with one of my deliverance mentors. The moment I told her, the Holy Spirit gave her direct understanding, and she knew exactly how to stop those demonic dreams. She explained to me that the enemy was trying to poison me by feeding me through my sleep. She instructed me to pray the following prayers during the midnight hours for six consecutive days. I followed her instructions, and for six days, I prayed around 11:00 p.m. or midnight. To the glory of God, these spiritual attacks stopped.

Prayers to Overcome Spiritual Attacks in Dreams

(Prayer Points originated by Damola Treasure Okenla)

1) Oh God, arise! Release "Goliath killing" stones to sanitize my dream life, in Jesus' name. (1 Samuel 17:49)

2) Blood of Jesus [repeat 7 times], sanitize my dreams. Neutralize any evil thing I have eaten and swallowed in the dream. My blood be neutralized by the power of the Holy Spirit, in Jesus' name. (Revelation 12:11)

3) I come against every evil power troubling my dream life, in Jesus' name. (Ephesians 6:12)

4) I come against every spirit of Balaam assigned to curse me in my dreams. I bind and silence you, in Jesus' name. (Numbers 22)

5) I come against every demonic mirror assigned to monitor my life through dreams, in Jesus' name. (Acts 16:17)

6) I come against every witchcraft power pursuing me through dreams. Disappear now, in Jesus' name. (Exodus 22:18)

7) I come against every satanic plan and investment against my dream life, in Jesus' name. (Hebrews 12:29)

8) I cancel and nullify any dream designed to alter the purpose of God for my life, in Jesus' name. (John 10:10)

9) I recover every good thing I have lost in the dream, in Jesus' name. (Joel 2:25)

CHAPTER SIX
No More Sexual Immorality

"My people are destroyed for lack of knowledge." – Hosea 4:6

I was first exposed to pornography as a child when I was watching television. A sexual scene that I viewed on television led me into years of bondage to pornography. I had not yet turned ten years old, but I was already addicted to pornography. This addiction transmuted into other sexual sins, later leading me to engage in masturbation and fornication. By the time I was in college, I became financially bound to the pornographic industry due to the purchases I was making to watch this evil content. I was in total captivity, and I knew it. I tried to stop the addiction on my own, but I could not. I was in deep bondage. Only by giving my life to Jesus was I able to gain freedom from a life of sexual immorality.

Right after giving my life to Christ, my addictions to pornography and masturbation were gone. I felt like my desire for these lusts had totally disappeared. I was yet to learn that the evil forces that held me bound to a life of sexual immorality could still come back to influence me. The truth is that I had agreed, through my past actions, to live a life of sexual immorality. The enemy was holding on to my agreement, which was like a contract I signed giving him and his evil forces the right to pervert my life. Yet, God did not allow them to prevail over me. Instead, God opened my spiritual eyes so that I would know the truth...and it all started with a dream.

Spirit Husband

"And you will know the truth, and the truth will set you free."

– John 8:32, NLT

I will never forget the day, or should I say the night, that one of my spiritual mentors gave me prayer points to pray concerning my marital destiny. She shared with me that she started praying for her marriage, husband and children while she was still single. Looking back, she realized how blessed her marriage and family was. She believed that praying in advance for her family played a major part in shaping how her life is today. I was blessed by her testimony, and I had seen her family and could attest that they were really blessed. So that evening, I prayed the marital prayer points she had given me. I had no idea that by making these prayers, God was about to open my spiritual eyes to see the major barriers facing my marital destiny.

That night, in a dream, I saw a man, who looked like my former boyfriend. This man was lying next to me in a bed, and he was forcing me to kiss him and he was being sexually abusive. Right after seeing this scene in the dream, I woke up in shock. Seeing a former boyfriend in a dream could have different meanings such as God warning us not to go back to old or bad habits. However, in my situation, the Holy Spirit made it very clear to me what that dream meant. Words could not describe how I felt. This man in my dream was a spirit husband.

I had heard of spirit husbands through mentors before and in church, but I never knew that I needed to deal with spirit husbands myself. I was completely ignorant, but God had finally revealed to me the truth. For the first time, I truly realized that I had issues in my foundations that I needed to address. I had heard through my mentors that spirit husbands or spouses are evil spiritual forces that try to destroy marital destinies and marriages. These spiritual forces are extremely possessive of the person influenced by them, which is why they do not want the individual to be in a relationship or marriage. Indeed, my marital destiny would suffer if I did not deal with what God had just revealed to me. I needed to know that truth in order to be set free.

From that dream onward, God began revealing to me many of the cracks in my foundations. As Jeremiah 33:3 states, as I called upon God, He answered me. He showed me great and mighty things, about which I had no idea.

"Father, I call upon You, visit every second of my life and reveal to me any issues in my foundations that I am unaware of. Deliver me where I need deliverance, in Jesus' name."

(Jeremiah 33:3)

Soul Ties

In the dream God gave me, I saw a man who looked like my former boyfriend. That man in the spiritual realm was a spirit husband whom I gave the right to influence my life, after engaging in sexual sins with my former boyfriend. More precisely, I had formed an ungodly soul tie. A *soul tie* is "an emotional link you create with someone in the spiritual realm." There are godly and ungodly soul ties. David and Jonathan in the Bible had a godly soul tie. They were best friend and loved each other in a godly manner. Indeed, God had blessed their friendship and their connection to one another (soul tie).

An ungodly soul tie, in the contrary, can be formed through illicit sexual relationships, unhealthy emotional relationships, or ungodly covenants with an organization or people. For instance, it is possible to develop ungodly soul ties with someone who has had negative control over us (unhealthy emotional relationship), such as abusive parents or spouse.

I was still tied spiritually with the people with whom I had been sexually engaged in the past. Ungodly soul ties between us had formed. Even though we had broken up in the physical realm, I was still tied to them through these ungodly soul ties. I now understood why I was still emotionally attached to my former boyfriend, with whom I had broken up with right before giving my life to Christ. There was still something linking me to him, unknown to me.

"And when Shechem the son of Hamor the Hivite, prince of the country, saw her, he took her and lay with her, and violated her. His soul was strongly attracted to Dinah the daughter of Jacob, and he loved the young woman and spoke kindly to the young woman. So Shechem spoke to his father Hamor, saying, "Get me this young woman as a wife." – Genesis 34:2-4

God first led me to understand soul ties, scripturally, through the story of Dinah, the daughter of Jacob, and Shechem, the man who raped her. After they had sexual intercourse, Shechem's soul became strongly attracted to Dinah's. A strong emotional tie and bond now existed between Shechem and Dinah. In fact, their souls were now tied through an ungodly soul tie.

Ungodly soul ties can result in spiritual marriage, which involves spirit spouses, and in some cases, spirit children. In my case, I had seen a spirit husband, and in later dreams, also spirit children. In one dream from God, I saw a spirit husband handing me a child to hold. That child was an ungodly spirit child. It was formed as a result of an ungodly soul tie. Sprit children are created to strengthen the soul tie and make it harder to break the link with spirit spouses. God was showing me that I needed to be delivered from spirit children as well as spirit husbands. These evil forces are able to gain access to our life through these ungodly soul ties.

A spirit husband or spirit wife is an evil spirit that comes in dream to sexually molest people. They also try to prevent people from having successful marital lives. That is why, God opened my spiritual eyes to see the spirit husband in my dream, as an answer to the prayers I had prayed concerning my marital destiny. God wanted me to totally break former ungodly soul ties in order to prevent their affecting my destiny. If spirit husbands, wives, or children are not addressed, they can cause serious issues in marriage, such as miscarriage, separation and even divorce. For single people, these evil spirits can cause delayed marriage or even prevent someone from getting married. But glory to God, through the blood of Jesus, we have the power to break free from every ungodly soul ties. Once we break an ungodly soul tie, the other person is also released from that soul tie.

Divine Connections[8], by Damola Treasure Okenla, one of my spiritual mentors, was a great source of knowledge for me to gain better understanding of ungodly soul ties and how the devil attacks marriages.

"Holy Spirit, reveal to me all the ungodly soul ties I have formed in my life, in Jesus' name." (Jeremiah 33:3)

Prayers to Break Ungodly Soul Ties

[Protective Prayers (pray out loud and with authority): *By the power and authority in the name of Jesus, I forbid any demonic force from manifesting in my life and in my environment. I bind and silence you, and I nail you to the cross, in Jesus' name. I cover all areas of my life and my surrounding in the blood of Jesus.]*

1) Father, forgive me for entering into ungodly soul ties with [mention name(s)] *by engaging in sexual sins* [and/or mention specific sins committed]. *I renounce and break my agreement with these sins. (Psalm 51)*

2) *I forgive and release everyone* [mention name(s)] *who influenced me to enter into these ungodly soul ties. I also choose to forgive and release myself from these sins. (Matthew 6:14)*

3) *I break every ungodly soul tie with* [mention name(s)], *in Jesus' name. I keep the Cross of Christ between us. I cancel the effect of such soul ties and every evil spiritual marriage with the blood of Jesus. (Genesis 34:2, 4; Colossians 2:14)*

4) *I command every spirit husband/wife and all evil spirits associated with such ungodly soul ties to leave me now, in Jesus' name. (Luke 10:19)*

5) *I cancel the powers of any token of such marriage: rings, wedding attires, certificates, and pictures, with the blood of Jesus. (Revelation 12:11)*

6) *I uproot every evil deposit, spirit children, magnets attached to these ungodly soul ties in my body, soul, or spirit with the blood of Jesus. (Matthew 15:13)*

7) *I cancel any evil and binding vows I have made concerning* [mention name(s)] [vows such that I will never love someone else like him or her, or mention other vows you made], *in Jesus' name.*

8) *I recover every good thing I have lost and I take back any part of my own person I have given through these soul ties, in Jesus' name. (Matthew 12:29)*

9) *Holy Spirit, fill me up so there would be no room for evil in my life. Baptize me and release upon me the grace to resist all sexual and other temptations, in Jesus' name (1 Corinthians 6:19, Luke 3:16, 2 Corinthians 12:9)*

10) *I come against every resistance to my prayers, in Jesus' name. I cover my body, soul, and spirit in the blood of Jesus (Revelation 12:7, Revelation 12:11)*

11) *I thank You, Lord, for answered prayers! (Luke 17:15, 16)*

After praying to break free of ungodly soul ties, we have to throw away any item that could still connect us to these people such as jewelry, special attires, or any binding documents.

The Strongman of Sexual Perversion

God taught me that my addiction to pornography, fornication, masturbation, and other sexual sins were all tied to one strongman. A *strongman* is "a spiritual force that has a stronghold upon one's life." A *stronghold* represents "a place that has been fortified." In fact, a stronghold is something that has been fortified in us and cannot easily break down. The more we engage in sexual sins, a stronghold forms. Once a stronghold has formed, it becomes very difficult to stop engaging in sins such as pornography or masturbation. These sins then become addictive. As a result, no matter how much one prays for deliverance, unless the stronghold is first broken, that person will remain addicted. If a stronghold is not dealt with, it can lead to more and more afflictions. In my case, it started with pornography, then masturbation and fornication. A stronghold had been fortified in me, and a strongman was in charge. Unless I first dealt with the strongman, the spirits attached to that strongman will keep coming back. The strongman behind sexual sins is called "the strongman of sexual perversion." Thanks be to God, no matter how many strongholds we may have formed in our life, Jesus is the stronger man who is able to destroy these holds (Luke 11:21, 22).

"Or how can one enter a strong man's house and plunder his goods, unless he first binds the strong man?" – Matthew 12:29

Matthew 12:29 explains that, for every stronghold, we need to first bind the strongman in prayer to break loose, which implies tie him down. In fact, a spiritual strongman enables multiple forces of darkness to operate together so they will be stronger at influencing people. When we bind, the strongman uniting these forces, we break their strength and powers. Most time when a strongman is involved, such as when someone is addicted to pornography, it is better to pray with an accountability partner (such as a Pastor, Minister, mentor, or prayer partner). In fact, it ensures the individual remains accountable to someone concerning that particular sin, which can help reduce the chances of relapse.

Deliverance brings great freedom as it removes the burden evil forces created in our life. Nonetheless, we need to ensure that before engaging in any deliverance, we fully understand the root of the problem—the specific door that was originally opened for the devil to operate in our life. We cannot skim through the surface. We have to ask the Holy Spirit to dig deep into our past to find out where the "bleeding" started in our lives. Since the time God taught me about inner healing, I have made it a habit to go through this process before going through any deliverance, especially if I know or if the Holy Spirit reveals to me the presence of an emotional wound. (See the "Prayers for Inner Healing" in the Prayer Points Index)

Prayers to Break Stronghold of Sexual Perversion

[Protective Prayers (pray out loud and with authority): *By the power and authority in the name of Jesus, I forbid any demonic force from manifesting in my life and in my environment. I bind and silence you, and I nail you to the cross, in Jesus' name. I cover all areas of my life and my surrounding in the blood of Jesus.]*

1) *Father, I repent for coming to agreement with the strongman of sexual perversion and the spirits of* [mention the ones that apply: lust, sexual fantasy , sexual defilement, pornography, masturbation, fornication, adultery, incest, rape, etc.] *I renounce and break all agreements I have made with these evil forces, in Jesus' name. (Psalm 51)*

2) *I forgive and release everyone* [mention name(s)] *who influenced me to engage in these sexual sins. I also forgive and release myself for committing these sins. (Matthew 6:14)*

3) *I take authority over the strongman of sexual perversion; I bind and cast you out, in Jesus' name. (Matthew 12:29)*

4) *I bind and cast out the spirit of* [one by one cast out the ones that apply: lust, sexual fantasy , sexual defilement, pornography, masturbation, fornication, adultery, incest, rape, etc.], *in Jesus' name. Never return again! (Mark 9:25)*

5) *Jesus, erase the initial imprint that came into my soul and the depth of my identity through my past sexual sins and encounters. Wipe the slate clean and break every ungodly craving. (Mark 5:25-29)*

6) *Holy Spirit, fill me up so there would be no room for evil in my life. Baptize me and release upon me the grace to resist all sexual temptations, in Jesus' name. (1 Corinthians 6:19, Luke 3:16, 2 Corinthians 12:9)*

7) *I come against every resistance to my prayers, in Jesus' name.*
I cover my body, soul, and spirit in the blood of Jesus (Revelation
12:7, Revelation 12:11)

[You can also apply some anointing oil on your forehead
(see page 73, Isaiah 10:27)].

8) *I thank You, Lord, for answered prayers! (Luke 17:15, 16)*

Sensual Dancing

"When an unclean spirit goes out of a man, he goes through dry
places, seeking rest, and finds none. Then he says, 'I will return to
my house from which I came.' And when he comes, he finds it
empty, swept, and put in order. Then he goes and takes with him
seven other spirits more wicked than himself, and they enter and
dwell there; and the last state of that man is worse than the first."

– Matthew 12:43-45

After being delivered from the forces of sexual perversion,
I had to stand strong and be vigilant. If there was anyone in
my life or anything that could lead me back to commit sexual
sins, I had to make sure to completely separated myself from
that person or thing. I had to stand strong in order to
maintain the freedom I had in Christ.

The Bible makes it clear that once we have been delivered
from an evil force, we should not open a door for that spirit
to control our lives again. If we go back to our sinful life such

as again engaging in masturbation or fornication, the condition we will be in will be worse than how we were before being delivered. We have to resist the temptation to go back to our old ways, and God has made the grace available for us to stand strong.

Some of the evil doorways we can open are not as clear as we think. I had made up my mind to never commit sexual sins again, and I made a vow of celibacy until marriage to God. I was convinced that the forces of sexual perversion would never be able to influence my life but, to my surprise, they came back—all because of *how I danced.*

As an unbeliever, I spent lots of nights partying at nightclubs and illicit bars. In fact, I first started going to nightclubs when I was only fifteen. As a result, the only type of dancing I truly knew was what I had learned in those places. I had learned how to dance very provocatively and sensually. Even after giving my life to Christ, my dancing remained the same. I knew that I had tendency to dance very sensually, which could cause others to lust over me, but I did not think it was an issue until God revealed to me that it was a big one.

"For My thoughts are not your thoughts, nor are your ways My ways," says the LORD. *- Isaiah 55:8*

One day I attended a special celebration, and on that day, I over-danced. I knew that I had danced too sensually, and I did not feel at peace in my spirit. The following night after this day of celebration, I had a dream that made me realize that my sensual dancing had reaffirm my agreement with the enemy and enabled him to influence me the more. In fact, in the dream, I saw an evil and perverted man entering the room where I was, and he said: *"I am not done with you. What was all this dancing about—the way you moved your body?"*

Through this "sensual dancing" episode, God taught me a very important lesson. After He delivers us from a particular condition, we have to stand strong and not open doors for the devil to pollute our lives. God had to correct me for the way I danced, and I had to accept the Lord's discipline. I had to unlearn a lot of my dancing. I prayed that God would teach me how to dance in a way that pleases Him and brings Him glory. I also prayed that God would make me aware of when I am dancing inappropriately.

It is very important as Christian that we make up our mind not to go back to our old ways. We should do our best to guard our victory in Christ. We should always pray for the grace to stand strong and that God will reveal to us if we are unwinkingly doing something wrong.

Ungodly Music

"All things are lawful for me, but not all things edify."

– 1 Corinthians 6:12

Besides my dancing, there was another surprising doorway I needed to be vigilant about. As an unbeliever, I was very attached to ungodly music. In fact, many of the songs I listened to were perverse in nature. After giving my life to Christ, the Holy Spirit convicted me concerning some of the songs I was listening to, but I was stubborn and resisted His instructions. In fact, I was not paying attention to the lyrics of these songs, which, for the most part, promoted lust and perversion. In fact, anytime I listened to these perverted songs, I was giving the devil rights to manipulate my thoughts, beliefs, and life. Yet, it was only after a particular incident that I finally yielded to the Holy Spirit.

"Don't copy the behavior and customs of this world, but let God transform you into a new person by changing the way you think. Then you will learn to know God's will for you, which is good and pleasing and perfect." – Romans 12:2, NLT

One day I attended a friend's party, and the DJ played all kinds of music. I danced to all of the songs played, and I did not even bother listening to the lyrics of these songs. Yet right after leaving the party, I felt a strong conviction that I should have paid attention to the lyrics of the songs. More than that, I knew something was wrong because I did not have peace at all. In fact, some of the songs played were extremely perverse.

That is when God started teaching me about music. If a song does not encourage, build up, or glorify God, then we should not listen or dance to it. We can also analyze how songs make us feel. After listening to a song, do we feel sexually aroused, violent, angry, depressed? Or do we feel encouraged, strengthen, joyful, motivated? These feelings could be an indication of the spirits attached to these songs. We have to analyze what the songs are saying, what they are promoting, and who they are glorifying. Spiritually, certain songs can have a strong impact on the person who listens to them. Some songs are tools in the hand of the enemy to pervert people's lives. If someone continuously listens to violent or lustful songs, it would not take long for that person to manifest violent or lustful behaviors. Singing is a form of worship. That is why, the Bible tells us in Psalm 22:3 that God dwells in the midst of praises of His people. Through singing praise song, we worship God and invite His presence into our lives. In the same way, when we sing songs that are evil in nature, we invite the presence of evil forces into our lives.

1) *Every evil spirit that has entered my life through ungodly music, wherever you are lodged in my body, soul or spirit, I uproot you with the blood of Jesus. (Psalm 18:45, Hebrews 12:29)*

2) *I block every evil gateway to my spirit that I have opened through ungodly music with the blood of Jesus. (Hebrews 4:12)*

3) *Father, uproot every desire in me to listen to ungodly music, in Jesus' name. (Matthew 15:13)*

4) *Holy Spirit, fill me up afresh and warn me whenever I listen or dance to an ungodly song.*

Guard My Mind

"Casting down arguments and every high thing that exalts itself against the knowledge of God, bringing every thought into captivity to the obedience of Christ." – 2 Corinthians 10:5

With years of watching pornography, listening to ungodly music, and engaging in sexual sins, my mind had been polluted by perverted thoughts. Now that I had been delivered, I had to guard my mind and not allow perverse thoughts and images to access my mind again. In today's society, we have to stand very strong against sexual immorality because it is everywhere. Through music, television and movies, the devil tries to expose us to a lot of perverse content, but we have to stay away from those.

Certain music and television programs can cause us to open doors to lust and perversion. Horror or witchcraft movies also open doors to many evil forces. They must completely be avoided. Satan tries to glamorize everything and make certain movies or music seem harmless. The truth is that he uses these avenues to infiltrate the lives of people.

We should stay far away from anything that can cause us to sin or tempt us through our eyes, ears, or in any other way. When deciding whether or not to watch a movie or a show, we should ask ourselves if Jesus would be able to sit down with us to watch it too. If Jesus cannot watch it, then we cannot watch it either. We should exercise the same discretion when deciding to go to certain places.

Having spent years going to nightclubs and illicit bars, I knew these were not appropriate places for me to hang out at with friends. The perverse activities that take place in those places can cause someone to completely fall into sexual and other bondages. We have to be very careful that we do not give the devil the right to control our lives, through what we see or the places we choose to go. I know of a particular man of God, who God led to minister in a nightclub, but I believe God knew that he would not fall into temptation while he was there. God will never tell us to take a path that will destroy us.

We have to always ask God for the grace to stay away

from temptations. What we visualize or listen to has the power to negatively impact our minds, and Satan knows this. The enemy continuously tries to attack us through our minds. Our mind is the doorway to our decision-making process. If the devil can get to our mind, he will be able to affect our decisions and cause us to do the wrong things. Satan always tries to plant evil thoughts in our minds, and if we are not careful, these evil seeds will grow and bear bad fruits in our lives. Whenever perverse thoughts come to our mind, we have to rebuke them out loud in Jesus' name (Zechariah 3:2).

I also found adding 2 Corinthians 10:5 and Philippians 4:8 to my list of daily confessions very helpful in controlling negative thoughts. We have to be very mindful concerning the state of our mind. Joyce Meyer wrote an amazing book, *Battlefield of the Mind*[9], which helped me understand how to guard my mind more effectively.

Prayers for a Renewed Mind

1) *I come against every mind-binding spirit, in Jesus' name. I forbid every demonic activity in my mind. (Luke 10:19)*

2) *I cast down every imagination and every high thing that exalts itself against the knowledge of God, and I bring every thought into captivity to the obedience of Christ, in Jesus' name. (2*

Corinthians 10:5)

3) *I declare and decree that I will think on things that are true, honorable, right, pure, lovely, and commendable, in Jesus' name! (Philippians 4:8)*

4) *Father, renew my mind and give me the mind of Christ, in Jesus' name! (1 Corinthians 2:16)*

CHAPTER SEVEN
Break Every Chain

"For this purpose the Son of God was manifested, that He might destroy the works of the devil." – 1 John 3:8

The famous proverb "Like father, like son" or "Like mother, like daughter" means that a child exhibits similar traits to his parents. These inherited traits can either be godly, such as when a child is generous and forgiving like his or her parents, or ungodly, such as when a child is always angry or becomes alcoholic like his parents. Just like blessings can pass down from a generation to another, sins can too.

"I lay the sins of the parents upon their children and

grandchildren; the entire family is affected—even children in the third and fourth generations." – Exodus 34:6, 7, NLT

As Exodus 34:7 explains, some children can suffer from the sins their ancestors committed. Specifically, if a particular sinful behavior is promoted in a home, it will greatly influence the behavior of children reared in that home. For instance, if a young girl grows up seeing her mother or both parents angry all of the time, she may begin to adopt such angry behavior as well. As a result, that young girl may also, just like her parents, come to agreement with the sin of anger. Indeed, when parents open the doors of their lives and their homes to the spirit of anger, their children find themselves in a harmful environment that welcomes anger. As a result, these children will be more likely to fall into this sin.

The only way to close the doors to the sins committed by parents is by ensuring that the children do not submit to these sins as well. Nevertheless, even if children try to resist the sins committed by their parents, the evil forces behind those sins will always have the right to influence that generation, unless that right is broken. The Bible confirms in Exodus 34: 6-7 that sins committed by parents can affect their offspring. These sins are therefore considered generational sins or curses. As Adam and Eve did by passing their sinful nature to us (Romans 5:12), when we submit to particular sins, without repenting of them, we pass those sins to our children.

This generational curse is illustrated in Joel 7:10–26 with the sin of Achan and its impact on his family. Joshua had gone to war, but the Lord did not grant them victory because some of the Israelites among them had committed great sins. In fact, Achan was an Israelite who had fought with Joshua in previous battles. Unlike most battles they won, God instructed the Israelites in Jericho not to take any of the spoils left behind because everything was considered accursed. Nevertheless, Achan coveted these spoils, which included fine garments and silver which he stole. As a result, the Israelites were unable to win subsequent battles until the sin and the sinner were identified. God exacted a severe judgment on Achan and his entire family for sinning against Him. Achan was stoned and burned to death along with his family. God could have forgiven Achan if he had repented, but he did not. His family may not have stolen anything, but they paid for the sin of Achan.

David's lineage was also affected when he committed adultery with Bathsheba, the wife of Uriah, and killed Uriah. David's case was a particular one because we can see in Psalms 51 that David repented wholeheartedly for his sins. God forgave him, which is why He did not kill David, or dethrone him as King of Israel. However, God still punished

David in order to teach the Israelites a lesson. God hates sin, and He certainly did not want the Israelites to think that adultery and other such sins were tolerated, especially by those who proclaim to be faithful children of God, such as what David had declared in the past. As we can see in 2 Samuel 12, David's firstborn with Bathsheba died. God also told David through the prophet Nathan that his other children will suffer because of his sins. Indeed, we read in the Bible that Tamar, David's daughter, was raped by her half-brother, Ammon. In order to obtain revenge, we also see that David's son, Absalom, killed Ammon for raping his sister Tamar. We also read in the Bible that in the same way David rebelled against God by sinning, his son, Absalom, rebelled against him by sleeping with ten of his concubines. We can conclude from David's example that his sins became curses in the lives of his children.

"You were dead because of your sins and because your sinful nature was not yet cut away. Then God made you alive with Christ, for he forgave all our sins. He canceled the record of the charges against us and took it away by nailing it to the cross."
– Colossians 2:13-14, NLT

Glory to the Lord, in Christ, we have been redeemed from all curses, including generational curses. Indeed, only Jesus can give us the strength to renounce and resist evil because He has broken the power of all generational sins and curses. In Jesus, we are new creatures, and we are no longer descendants of evil. So when we accept Jesus as our Lord and Savior and break our agreements with evil, the generational power of sin is broken over our lives and the lives of our descendants. Generational curses do not apply to a child of God submitted to Him. Unlike the children of David who suffered for their father's sins, the people who give their lives to Jesus will not pay for the sins of their parents or ancestors, unless these people have already succumbed to these same sins without repenting of them. It is therefore very important to understand that generational curses will continue in a family line only if the children, even if they are Christians, commit the same sins as their parents. Curses only work against those, including Christians, who rebel against God. That's why Paul tells us in Ephesians 4:27: "Leave no room for the devil." Indeed, when we, as Christians, commit a sin without renouncing it (rebellion), we submit ourselves to the impure forces attached to that sin, and we give them the right to continue tempting us and our descendants. The forces attached to these sins will continue to influence our descendants, unless we renounce our covenant with them and break their hold over our lives.

In my walk with the Lord, I have make mistakes and I have fallen, but it is very important for me to stay honest with God. Temptations are everywhere and God knows it. We must be humble in order to let God show us where we need help. That's why it's so important for me to have accountability partners that I can confide in when I make mistakes. Jesus gives us the strength to overcome all temptations, and we must remain strong as Christians in order not to allow the devil to pollute our lives or our descendants. In Christ, we have the power to give our generation the most beautiful blessings instead of curses!

We must ask the Holy Spirit to reveal to us the generational sins we have, consciously or unconsciously, succumbed to. In some families, generational curses can be bitterness, incest, pornography, division, divorce, depression, false religion, excessive drinking, and others. We must always be vigilant and determined never to create agreements with the devil, in order to remain under the shelter and protection of the Lord (James 4: 7).

Prayers for Freedom from Habitual Sins

[Protective Prayers (pray out loud and with authority): *By the power and authority in the name of Jesus, I forbid any demonic force from manifesting in my life and in my environment. I bind and silence you, and I nail you to the cross, in Jesus' name. I cover all areas of my life and my surrounding in the blood of Jesus.]*

1) Father, I confess my sins and the sins of my ancestors of [mention the sin(s) and ungodly pattern(s)]. *Forgive us, Lord.* (Ephesians 1:7)

2) I forgive and release my ancestors, myself, [mention others] for committing these sins and for the resulting consequences in my life and generation. (Matthew 6:14)

3) I renounce and break my agreement with the sins of [mention the sin(s)], and I cancel the resulting curses from my life and the lives of my descendants, in Jesus' name. (Colossians 2:14, Mark 9:25)

4) I break and cancel every evil link with my parents and ancestors with the blood of Jesus. (Psalms 68:1)

5) Father, sever any demonic links between my soul and spirit, and cleanse me of everything bad I inherited or agreed with in my life, in Jesus' name. (Hebrews 4:12)

6) Holy Spirit, fill me up so there would be no room for evil in my life, in Jesus' name. (1 Corinthians 6:19)

7) Holy Spirit, renew my mind so that I would no longer follow the ungodly patterns of my past. (Romans 12:1-2)

8) I come against every resistance to my prayers, in Jesus' name. I cover my body, soul, and spirit in the blood of Jesus. (Revelation

12:7, Revelation 12:11)

[You can also apply some anointing oil on your forehead (see page 73, Isaiah 10:27)].

9) I thank You, Lord, for answered prayers! (Luke 17:15, 16)

Breaking Free from Ungodly Covenants

"And have no fellowship with the unfruitful works of darkness, but rather expose them." – Ephesians 5:11

While I was a student in the university, I joined a business fraternity. At the time, I was still an unbeliever, and I had no idea that anything could be wrong with joining a fraternity or a sorority. I had enjoyed my experience and the people I had met within the organization. In fact, our business fraternity did not practice hazing, so I did not see anything wrong with being a member. However, after giving my life to Christ, God used one of my Christian mentors to reveal to me the truth behind certain fraternities and sororities. She explained to me that I had possibly entered into an ungodly covenant during the rituals we performed at initiation. A *covenant* is "a formal and binding agreement (written or spoken) between two or more parties." There are both godly (Hebrews 12:24) and ungodly covenants (Exodus 34:7).

From the moment my mentor spoke to me about ungodly covenants, I felt a certain discomfort within me. The Bible tells us that *"you shall know the truth, and the truth shall make you free...."* After talking to my mentor, I felt as if the Holy Spirit had spotlighted an area of my life He wanted me to examine. I believe the discomfort came from my trying to resist the conviction of the Holy Spirit.

The Holy Spirit is gentle, and He does not force us to believe anything without understanding. I prayed that God will make it clear to me concerning the truth behind fraternities and sororities and give me a teachable heart. That is when the Holy Spirit reminded me of what had happened during the initiation process when I joined that business fraternity.

At initiation, we went into a dark room lit only by candlelight. I was asked different questions by members of the business fraternity. Once we were selected to join the organization, a specific ritual followed. A secret sign members made with their hands when they greeted was also revealed. We sang the hymn of the fraternity and made an oath with the organization. We were also given shirts and a stole, and we signed an agreement as new members.

The freemasons also have similar rituals in their initiation process such as exchanging signs and making oaths. The father of one pastor I know well was very involved in freemasonry. In fact, he held a high rank within the organization. She told me that one of the oaths her dad had made involved his never leaving the organization. If he did, he would suffer a very cruel death. The sad part of the story is that her dad not only lived in tremendous bondage most of his life but he also died of a very cruel death as he had confessed under the oath.

Even though I did not have to make such oath when I joined my organization, I did not know the types of oaths the original founders made or those higher-ranked members made concerning the organization as a whole, which will have an effect on all its members.

"If anyone thoughtlessly takes an oath to do anything, whether good or evil (in any matter one might carelessly swear about) even though they are unaware of it, but then they learn of it and realize their guilt— when anyone becomes aware that they are guilty in any of these matters, they must confess in what way they have sinned."

– Leviticus 5:4, 5, NIV

As I started reflecting on what had happened at the initiation to join this business fraternity, I realized that something was wrong. I was unsure as to what type of oath and agreement I had made with them in the first place. I knew I was somehow bound to the organization through the oath and agreement I had signed. This fraternity was not founded on Christian principles, and I was not sure if all of their foundational principles were godly ones. The fact that I also had no idea what the signs made during initiation meant troubled me all the more. I had no peace at all, and the very fact I made an actual oath troubled me. I did not want to be under any type of ungodly covenant.

Not long after, God brought some clarity through a dream in which I saw myself with other members of that business fraternity. We were prisoners in a basement, darkness surrounded us, and we could not escape. That dream was enough to confirm my doubts. I knew God had sent my mentor to warn me and to ensure I break the covenant I had taken with this business fraternity.

Even though that business fraternity did good things for the community and its members (like freemasons do), I knew God had a good reason for telling me to leave. He knows all truth, and nothing is hidden from Him. I contacted the fraternity to tell them I was leaving, and I would no longer continue with them. I also prayed to renounce and break my association with them in the spirit realm. I threw away the shirts and stole I had been given so that nothing would be binding me to them. If you are part of a fraternity or a sorority, I encourage you to seek God for the truth concerning the organization, especially if you made an oath.

"The Son radiates God's own glory and expresses the very
character of God, and he sustains everything by the mighty power of
his command. When he had cleansed us from our sins, he sat down
in the place of honor at the right hand of the majestic God in
heaven. This shows that the Son is far greater than the angels, just
as the name God gave him is greater than their names... And when
he brought his supreme Son into the world, God said, "Let all of
God's angels worship him." - Hebrews 1:3-4,6

In addition to this business fraternity, I prayed to
disconnect myself from any ungodly organizations I had ever
joined and with which I had unknowingly made ungodly
covenants in the past. One was made with the Jehovah
Witnesses, the religion in which many of my family members
were reared. I had attended many of their meetings while
growing up, and I wanted to make sure I broke all ties with
this organization as well. In fact, through prayers and
intensive study of the Bible concerning Jehovah's Witnesses,
the Holy Spirit explained to me how they differed from the
Truth.

Jehovah's Witnesses do not believe that Jesus is God, but
they believe that Jesus is the Son of God and an angel, not
God himself. Moreover, they do not believe in the concept of
the Trinity. The big problem is that not believing that Jesus is
God, and rather believing that He is only an angel, reduces

our relationship with Him and the way we see Him. The Bible clearly explains to us in Revelation 7:11 and Hebrews 1:14 that angels were created to worship God and to serve us, the children of God. Jesus has a much higher role than angels, who are servants of the children of God. This is why the Bible says in Hebrews 1: " This shows that the Son [Jesus] is far greater than the angels, just as the name God gave him is greater than their names." Now that I have clarified why Jesus is not an angel, I will explain why Jesus is God and how to understand the concept of the Trinity.

I also struggled after giving my life to Christ with the concept of the Trinity. How can God be three persons in one? How can God be a human being (Jesus)? I encourage you to always seek for the truth. No matter your struggle with the Bible or biblical concepts, I encourage you to pray that God will give you understanding so that you will stand strong and be secure in your salvation.

Do not be intimidated if people ask you difficult questions about the Bible. Seek answers in the study of the Bible; God will not fail you, and He will show you the way to the truth. God is not the author of confusion but of peace. How the Holy Spirit gave me a comprehensive understanding of the Trinity, even though I was a very young Christian is amazing. God saw that I was longing for the truth—not a religion. In addition to praying for understanding, I took advantage of

Bible commentaries, which are available online for free for us to gain deeper understanding of the Bible.

"You must have the same attitude that Christ Jesus had. Though he was God, he did not think of equality with God as something to cling to. Instead, he gave up his divine privileges; he took the humble position of a slave and was born as a human being. When he appeared in human form, he humbled himself in obedience to God and died a criminal's death on a cross."

– Philippians 2:5-8

The word *trinity* is a Latin-based word, which means the "state of being threefold." The word *trinity* is actually not mentioned in the Bible but has been adopted by Christians to describe God as three persons: God the Father, God the Son, God the Holy Spirit. The word *trinity* is the best fit in the dictionary to describe God, which I believe is why the word is used instead of always repeating "Father, Son, Holy Spirit."

In John 3:16, the Bible explains how God gave His only begotten Son to save us. This Scripture is sufficient to prove the fact that God is a Father in nature. Most people usually see God as a Father, so grasping this concept is easier. When Christians refer to God as "God the Son," the concept becomes more controversial.

Philippians 2:5-8 explains how Jesus did not did not cling

to His equality with God but gave up His divine privileges and humbled Himself in obedience to God. These Scriptures make it clear that Jesus was equal to God. How can someone be equal to God without being God as well?

To add to these thoughts, I have no doubt God would humble Himself to save me from my sins because God is love. His very nature is love. He did not create us to suffer and die due to the consequences of our sins. He wanted us to live for eternity with Him. If a loving father sees his children drowning in the sea, he will run to rescue them. Whether the father is a president or a king matters little. Love sacrifices. Jesus gave up His divine privilege and took on a human nature to rescue us from our sins. He could have remained fully divine but because He is love, He sacrificed Himself for us. Philippians 2:5-8 confirms that Jesus is God.

Acts 5:3-11 shares an account of the couple Ananias and Sapphira who lied to the apostles concerning the sale of their property. Peter said to Ananias, *"Why has Satan filled your heart to lie to the Holy Spirit…You have not lied to men but to God."* In this passage, Peter confirmed that the Holy Spirit is God. He could have asked "Why did you lie to the Father?" but Peter asked why he had lied to the Holy Spirit.

Before Jesus left earth, He told His disciples that He would send the Holy Spirit to help them. In fact, when we give our lives to Christ, the Holy Spirit comes to live inside of us. God promised never to leave or forsake us, so I am not surprised that He will make sure that we, His precious children, carry His presence wherever we go.

Finally, some argue that God does not have to be one being but could be many. For instance, the Father, the Son, and the Holy Spirit could be multiple Gods. Yet God declares very clearly in Isaiah 43:10-11 that *"Before Me there was no God formed, Nor shall there be after Me. I, even I, am the LORD, And besides Me there is no savior."* This passage confirms clearly that if the Father, the Son (Jesus), the Holy Spirit are all Gods, then they must be One. Both Genesis 1:26 and 3:22 also confirm the unity in the Trinity since God identifies Himself as One by using the word "us." In our finite minds, understanding this concept could be difficult, but God is not at our level; He is infinite. Quantum physics proved how atomic particles could be in an infinite number of places at once, which can be difficult to believe yet is true. Then why couldn't God be three in One? God is the Creator of the entire universe so we cannot expect Him to be like us. His nature is far superior to ours.

"But there were also false prophets in Israel, just as there will be false teachers among you. They will cleverly teach destructive heresies and even deny the Master who bought them. In this way,

they will bring sudden destruction on themselves."

- 2 Peter 2:1 (NLT)

We have to be very careful of false religions or teachers. I encourage you to always pray for a discerning spirit so that you will not be deceived in your knowledge of God. Jesus is *"the way, the truth, and the life."* He does not want us to follow Him blindly. We should never be fearful to ask questions concerning the Bible. When we have doubts, we should ask the Holy Spirit in prayer for clarification and seek for answers to our questions (through the Bible or biblical teachers).

I usually do not like to refer to my faith in Jesus as a religion. Jesus is my life not a mere religion to me. I do not want to live a religious life; rather, I want to live knowing the truth. I pray the Holy Spirit guides you so that you will never fall to false teachings of the Bible or that are against biblical truth. Even if you do not believe in the Bible, I encourage you to pray that God will make Himself real to you and guide you to the truth.

When I broke my agreement with the Jehovah's Witnesses, I made sure to throw away their Bible. Their Bible, the New World Translation of the Holy Scriptures, did not contain God's truth so I no longer wanted to use it as a reference.

Prayers to Break Ungodly Covenants

[Protective Prayers (pray out loud and with authority): *By the power and authority in the name of Jesus, I forbid any demonic force from manifesting in my life and in my environment. I bind and silence you, and I nail you to the cross, in Jesus' name. I cover all areas of my life and my surrounding in the blood of Jesus.*]

1) *Father, I thank You for Jesus, the mediator of the new covenant I have with You. (Hebrews 9:15)*

2) *Holy Spirit, reveal to me any ungodly covenants I have made in the past, knowingly or unknowingly, in Jesus' name. (John 14:26)*

3) *Father, forgive me for every ungodly covenant into which I have entered knowingly or unknowingly with* [mention the organizations' names]. *I renounce every ungodly covenant I made with these organizations, in Jesus' name. (Leviticus 5:5)*

4) *I forgive and release* [mention names] *for contributing to my entering into these ungodly covenants. I also forgive and release myself for these sins. (Matthew 6:14)*

5) *I break every ungodly covenant with* [mention the organizations' names], *with the blood of Jesus. I cancel the effects of such covenants over my life, in Jesus' name. (Revelation 12:11)*

6) *I command every evil spirit behind every ungodly covenant I made with* [mention the organizations' names] *to leave me now*

and loose their hold over my life, in Jesus' name. (Luke 10:19)

7) *I consume any item linking me to these organizations: stole, rings, special attires, certificates, and pictures, with the fire of the Holy Spirit, in Jesus' name. (Deuteronomy 4:24)*

8) *I declare my freedom from all ungodly covenants. The blood of Jesus has redeemed me, and I am free! Thank You, Lord, for answered prayers! (Galatians 3:13)*

Breaking Free from Idols

"Ephraim is joined to idols; leave him alone!" – Hosea 4:17, NIV

An *idol* is "anything or anyone to whom a person devotes his or her worship, trust and attention." As Hosea 4:17 informs us, by joining ourselves to idols we prevent God from fellowshipping with us. God is a jealous God, and He will not share His glory with anyone or anything. God will not share us with other gods to which we may have yielded our lives. We cannot be joined to idols and remain in Christ.

People use many things, thinking that they are signs of God's protection when truly these things are idols taking God's place in their lives. For instance, using rings, amulets, rosaries, scapulars, colored candles, and religious objects for protection or good luck are all idolatrous practices. These objects are not God. Unfortunately, some religions teach people to use them as a way to connect to God or to be protected by Him. The only way to God is through Jesus—not objects. We must be willing to break free from idols in order to develop a relationship with God. Idols can also be men or women whom we worship and substitute for God in our life. We have to ask the Holy Spirit to reveal any idols in our life.

"For there is one God and one Mediator between God and men, the Man Christ Jesus." – 1 Timothy 2:5

Another form of idolatry includes people's praying to angels, saints, statues, images, or anyone besides God. Our prayers should be addressed to God alone. Praying to saints or consulting the dead is evil. The only intermediary between us and God the Father is Jesus. The Bible is clear on the fact that once someone dies, the person is absent from the body and present with the Lord. We should not seek to pray or make any contact with the dead. They are completely disconnected from this world. Black magic, fortune-tellers, witches, wizards, and all who claim to communicate with the dead are occult practitioners. They have Satan and evil forces as the source of their information—not God.

The Bible also makes it clear that we should not worship angels, who are only here to serve us and should not be revered or worshipped (Hebrews 1:14). After God used an angel in the book of Revelation to show John the things that were to come in the end times, John fell down to worship that angel (Revelation 22:8, 9). However, that angel made it clear to John that he should not worship him. The angel told him that he was simply his servant and that he should worship only God.

"Father, reveal to me the idols in my life and grant me the grace to completely let go of them. Uproot these idols from my heart, in Jesus' name." (Ezekiel 14:3, 4)

CHAPTER EIGHT
Spiritual Warfare

"To everything there is a season, a time for every purpose under heaven: ... a time of war" – Ecclesiastes 3:1, 8

---

*S*piritual warfare represents a time when believers engage in a spiritual war against evil. During these times we fight against the forces opposing our destiny. These opposing forces are not actually people but spiritual forces of darkness. They are the ones influencing people to do evil and the ones we should fight against—not other human beings. The Bible says in Ephesians 6:12, *"We do not wrestle against flesh and blood, but against principalities, against powers, against the rulers of the darkness of this age, against spiritual hosts of wickedness in the heavenly places."*

Spiritual warfare can occur for many reasons such as when

we are praying for healing and deliverance (Matthew 17:21), interceding for people (Daniel 10:12-13), at the edge of a breakthrough or when we are rising to a new level in destiny (1 Corinthians 16:9). When we go through spiritual warfare, the devil does everything to wrestle with us and attack us. In the physical realm, he can attack us through people, our finances, our health, our relationships, and more. He tries to fight back to stop our prayers from being answered.

God has given me the gift of discerning of spirits (1 Corinthians 12:10), which has enabled me to detect when evil forces are behind certain activities. For instance, during a season when I was fasting and praying concerning a particular issue in my life, some people who were close to me started attacking me for no real reason. I knew the devil was behind these attacks. Sometimes, these people were unbelievers or even believers, but they were unaware that the enemy was influencing them to attack me (Matthew 18:7).

In the spiritual realm, I have also experienced attacks during spiritual warfare. For instance, I have sometimes felt evil forces attacking me, and more specifically, pressing me down when I am asleep. As Ephesians 6:12 mentions, we do not wrestle against the things we see when we go through spiritual warfare, but against the forces of darkness in the spiritual world.

We may also experience attacks after we have been

delivered from an unclean spirit (evil force). The Bible tells us in Luke 11:24 that when an unclean spirit has gone out of a person, it looks for a place to find rest and when he does not find it, that evil spirit tries to return to the person it came from. In my case, God had taken me through a lot of deliverance, and I knew from that Scripture that some of the attacks I was experiencing in my sleep came from evil forces that were trying to come back to influence my life.

Whenever these attacks occur, we have to rebuke these forces strongly (such as saying, *"I rebuke you, in Jesus' name!"*) as they no longer have any right to afflict us. As long as we have broken our agreement with them, they have no right to disturb us. However, if we dabble in our former sins, we are opening doors for them to attack us. For this reason, resisting the devil and not going back to our old ways is very important in order for these evil forces never to trouble us again. We have to stand strong and rebuke the enemy until these spiritual attacks stop. Once the enemy knows that we have made up our minds and will never go back to our old ways, he will leave us alone.

I also went through strong spiritual warfare while interceding for other people. In fact, when I was praying intensely for the salvation of some of my family members, the devil tried to retaliate. God showed me that when we pray for others, some of their spiritual warfare can transfer to us. In

Daniel 10:13, Daniel experienced a strong spiritual warfare while interceding for his Jewish people. Nevertheless, those intimidations should not stop us from praying for others. We have to rebuke intimidation and fear when they come.

Many people with great destinies in the Bible experienced great warfare. Satan had already purposed to destroy Moses before he was even born. In Exodus 1:16, the king of Egypt had given instructions to midwives to kill every male child. The ultimate goal of the enemy was to destroy Moses because he was a child of destiny, but his plan failed. The same thing happened to Jesus, whose parents had to flee from their town to prevent King Herod from killing baby Jesus (Matthew 2:16). Joseph and Daniel were also men of God with great destiny whom the enemy tried to abort unsuccessfully (Genesis 37:20, Daniel 6:16).

The greater the plans of God for our life sometimes means the greater the warfare. We should not be discouraged when we go through spiritual warfare and wonder why God is allowing it to happen. On the contrary, we should dig into His Word, the Bible, to figure out what are the weapons of spiritual warfare at our disposal to counterattack the tactics of the enemy. Jesus promised never to leave us comfortless. He sent the Holy Spirit to live inside every believer for guidance and comfort.

Weapons for Spiritual Warfare

"Therefore take up the whole armor of God, that you may be able

to withstand in the evil day, and having done all, to stand. Stand

therefore, having girded your waist with truth, having put on the

breastplate of righteousness, and having shod your feet with the

preparation of the gospel of peace; above all, taking the shield of

faith with which you will be able to quench all the fiery darts of the

wicked one. And take the helmet of salvation, and the sword of the

Spirit, which is the word of God; praying always with all prayer

and supplication in the Spirit, being watchful to this end with all

perseverance and supplication for all the saints"

– Ephesians 6:13–18

Christ has won the victory on the Cross for us, and God
has placed everything at our disposal for us to be victorious
in all spiritual warfare (Colossians 2:14, 15). There is no
warfare that we cannot overcome in our walk with Christ
(Philippians 4:13). Nonetheless, my journey to understanding
the weapons at my disposal was long. In fact, for couple of
years after giving my life to Christ, I was experiencing severe
attacks in my sleep. A time came when I could not take any
more attacks, so I dug into God's Word and truth. I started
searching into the Bible to find all the weapons of protection
I could use to defend myself. I knew I had to stand strong on

God's Word concerning my sleep. God gives His beloved sweet sleep, and I could not take any more restless nights (Job 22:28).

God did not want me to be tormented while sleeping. He wanted my sleep to be peaceful so that I would be able to receive revelations from Him through my dreams. The devil did everything to hinder me from receiving instructive dreams from God at night. That is why I had to exercise my authority in Christ and discover how I could stand strong against the enemy's perpetual attacks in my sleep. I could not become intimidated or stop praying whenever I experienced those attacks. I had to pray that God would give me the heart of a lion (Proverbs 28:1) and make me bolder when I go through spiritual warfare. Through the spiritual attacks I experienced, God started teaching me how to effectively shield myself and stand strong.

The Sword of the Spirit

"...the sword of the Spirit, which is the word of God."

– Ephesians 6:17

As Christians, we must be well acquainted with the weapons of warfare God has placed at our disposal in order to properly resist evil forces. One of the most powerful weapons we can use to combat them is the Word of God, the

Bible. The Word of God is "sharper than any two-edged sword" (Hebrews 4:12). For whatever problems we are going through, at least one Scripture in the Bible will yield a solution. Nothing under the sun is new. We can find solutions to any problems we go through in the Bible.

When I was going through severe attacks in my sleep, I started praying the same prayer of deliverance that David prayed in his psalm. Using Psalm 143 and Psalm 59, I cried to God to intervene and deliver me from these evil trespassers of my sleep. Also, in order to arrest these evil forces coming to attack me in my dream, I memorized Colossians 2:14 and 15, praying it out loud as a shield against them. Satan does not like to hear that Christ has triumphed over him and that he is defeated. That is why the Bible says in Ephesians 10 that the Word of God is a sword that cuts off the power of evil. The enemy cannot nullify the power of the Word of God. Knowing the Scriptures well is important, especially those that apply to a particular situation we are trying to address.

Pray in the Spirit

"Praying always with all prayer and supplication in the Spirit."

– Ephesians 6:18

In addition to using the Word of God, I started praying more intensely in the Spirit. Speaking in the Spirit or speaking in tongues is a spiritual gift given by the Holy Spirit (1 Corinthians 12:10). When we speak in the Spirit, we speak directly to God (1 Corinthians 14:2), and the Holy Spirit intercedes for us. In fact, when we do not know what to pray, the Holy Spirit, Himself, intercedes for us when we speak in the Spirit (Romans 8:26). Through speaking in tongues, the Holy Spirit prays the exact prayers we need, and answers to our problems are being released. Revelations come when we speak in the Spirit. In addition, when we speak in the Spirit, we are able to intercede, not only for ourselves, but also others. Since the Holy Spirit is God, He knows exactly what we need to pray about, so praying often in the Spirit is important. By praying in tongues, we pray God's perfect will for our lives. The Bible also states that when we speak in tongues, we are strengthened (1 Corinthians 14:4). As a result, our body, soul, and spirit become strengthened and fortified. Speaking in the Spirit enables us to receive the strength we need for any situation we face. We can receive the gift of speaking in tongues by asking God directly in faith (1 Corinthians 14:1) or by having a spiritual leader lay hands on us (Acts 19:6).

Speaking in tongues is one evidence that we have received an infilling of the Holy Spirit (Acts 2:4), which is also referred to as "the baptism of the Holy Spirit." The *infilling* of the

Holy Spirit is different than the *indwelling* of the Holy Spirit, which occurs when we give our lives to Christ. In fact, the Holy Spirit lives insides every believer (1 Corinthians 3:16) but through the infilling of the Holy Spirit, a believer is given extraordinary power to witness for Christ (Acts 1:8). During spiritual warfare, praying in the Spirit more often is important as the Holy Spirit will pray for us to overcome the battle. God encouraged me to pray in the Spirit at least one hour per day. We can easily achieve that goal by praying fifteen minutes in the Spirit four times a day.

The Blood of Jesus

> *"And they overcame him by the blood of the Lamb."*
>
> *– Revelation 12:11*

Whenever we enter into spiritual warfare through prayers, such as praying for deliverance or interceding for people, we should always cover ourselves in the blood of Jesus. As a young believer, I started experiencing severe attacks in my sleep after I would intercede for people. One of my Christian mentors, who has been a leader in the ministry of deliverance, explained to me that I needed to shield myself in the blood of Jesus before I engaged in spiritual warfare.

> *"being watchful to this end with all perseverance and supplication for all the saints."* – Ephesians 6:18

After experiencing resistance while interceding for other people, God revealed to me that others' warfare can transfer to us. In fact, when we are praying for people, we do not know the evil forces that are holding them bound or the forces that are working against them. Nonetheless, we should not stop praying for others as our own deliverance may be dependent on our obedience to the Word of God, which tells us to pray for all people (1 Timothy 2:1). In Job 42:10, we see that Job's own warfare ended after he prayed for his friends. He experienced the recovery of all that he had lost after praying for other people. We have to come to the throne of God boldly when we are praying, forbidding the spirits of fear and intimidation to take root in our heart. We must also follow the leading of the Holy Spirit when He instructs us to pray for people.

Nehemiah and the people who joined him to rebuild the walls of Jerusalem also had to overcome fear. Nehemiah risked the comfort he had in the palace as the king's cupbearer to ensure that the walls of Jerusalem were rebuilt. He had a burden for the sufferings of his people and did not mind losing his own comfort to defend others. In Nehemiah 4:14, when faced with great opposition, Nehemiah had to encourage his people not to be afraid of their adversaries but to continue fighting for their families:

"...Don't be afraid of the enemy! Remember the Lord, who is great and glorious, and fight for your brothers, your sons, your daughters, your wives, and your homes!" – Nehemiah 4:14, NLT

In the same token, we cannot stop praying for others for fear that evil forces will attack us. We are to be bold and stand in the gap for our loved ones. We have to keep reminding ourselves that we are on the winning side. Christ has already given us the victory! In fact, by covering ourselves in the blood of Jesus, we are able to protect ourselves from the backlashes of the enemy. Whenever we are interceding for people who are going through strong spiritual warfare, we can pray the following prayer to protect ourselves:

"I bring the full work of Christ on the Cross between me and [mention the name of the people you are interceding for]. *I command their human spirits bound back to their bodies, and their sins and warfare bound to the throne of Christ. I forbid them to transfer to me, in Jesus' name."* (Colossians 2:14, Daniel 10:13)

During times of spiritual warfare covering our health, home, family, friends, relationships, finances, business, career, ministry, possessions and any other thing or person that is close to us in the blood of Jesus is wise. In fact, if the devil cannot attack us directly, he will try to attack the people and things that are dear to us, but the blood of Jesus is a strong shield against him.

God's Consuming Fire

"For our God is a consuming fire." – Hebrews 12:29

Another powerful weapon the devil and his evil forces cannot tolerate is the consuming fire of God, which burns up anything unholy. The Bible explains in Zechariah 2:5 how the Lord had planned to protect Jerusalem by being a wall of fire around the city. God's fire can protect, but it can also destroy. The Bible tells of God's raining down His fire from heaven to destroy Sodom and Gomorrah (Genesis 19:24). His fire is enough to terrify and destroy our enemies, for God is a consuming fire. That is why, I started asking God to make me, my family, and my home untouchable flames of fire (Hebrews 1:7). Before going to bed, I usually ask God to surround me with His fire so that no evil will come near me during my sleep. Evil forces cannot resist the consuming fire of God!

Angels

"For he will order his angels to protect you wherever you go. They will hold you up with their hands so you won't even hurt your foot on a stone." – Psalm 91:11-12, NLT

God assigns His angels to protect us both during the day and at night. The Bible also states in Hebrews 1:14 that angels are present to serve us. As a result, we can command the angels that God assigns over us to fight any battle erected against us. After experiencing very fierce spiritual battles in my sleep, I started studying more about angels.

In Daniel 10:13, after Daniel fasted and prayed for 21 days, the prince of Persia, an evil principality controlling the court of Persia, was withholding the answers to Daniel's prayer. Daniel was facing strong spiritual warfare, and the angel assigned to fight for him experienced strong resistance from the prince of Persia. Yet a higher-ranked angel, Michael, one of the chief angelic princes, was sent to help him conquer this evil principality. After reading the story of Daniel, I started praying for God to send more angelic reinforcements to help me conquer the spiritual warfare I was facing. God can send us legions of angels to fight for us if we ask Him (Matthew 26:53).

Praise and Worship

"Now when they began to sing and to praise, the LORD set
ambushes against the people of Ammon, Moab, and Mount Seir,
who had come against Judah; and they were defeated."

– 2 Chronicles 20:22

Praising and worshipping God during times of spiritual warfare is a powerful weapon we can use against the devil. When we exalt and magnify God during adverse moments, it not only strengthens our faith, but it also causes God to intervene on our behalf. In fact, praising God brings down His presence into our lives as God inhabits the praises of His people (Psalm 22:3). Praises confuse the enemy and repel his presence in our life.

Satan cannot tolerate listening to praises given to God and flees at the presence of God in our life. Praise brings down the power of God and causes Him to manifest His power through our praise. Many times in the Bible battles were won because the people of God praised Him (2 Chronicles 20:22; Acts 16:25, 26; Joshua 6:20). I have experienced great peace during strong spiritual warfare because I decided to praise God through the storm.

Praying Partners

"Though one may be overpowered by another, two can withstand him. And a threefold cord is not quickly broken."

– Ecclesiastes 4:12

There is power in number. Many times when I faced strong spiritual warfare, I sought the help of other believers. I asked them to stand in the gap by praying for me. When

Peter was facing strong spiritual warfare and imprisoned by King Herod, the church prayed for him. At the time, Christians were being arrested and persecuted severely. James, the brother of John, was even put to death. Peter was also about to face death, but the church interceded for him. The battle that the church was facing was very fierce, and in order for Peter to gain his deliverance, others had to stand in the gap for him.

Some battles are not meant to be fought alone. It is wise to have other believers agree with us in prayer when we are going through spiritual warfare. We can even ask God in prayer to raise men to intercede for us. There is great power in number, and we can tap into that power during spiritual warfare!

Spiritual Warfare We Should Avoid

"But even Michael, one of the mightiest of the angels, did not dare accuse the devil of blasphemy, but simply said, 'The Lord rebuke you!' (This took place when Michael was arguing with the devil about Moses' body.)." – Jude 1:9, NLT

One of my mentor encouraged me to read the book *Needless Casualties of War*[11] by John Paul Jackson. This book provides powerful insights concerning the types of spiritual warfare in which we should not engage as Christians. In this book, the author shares many stories of Christians who were severely attacked after they tried binding and casting out territorial spirits (powers reigning over regions) in their communities. For example, the prince of Persia mentioned in Daniel 10:13 was a principality over the Persian kingdom. The goal of this principality was to negatively influence the Persian rulers in order to advance the kingdom of darkness in that region. Concerning principalities or territorial powers, we should not *bind* or *come against* these forces unless we have received clear confirmations from God that we can do so. Just like the angel in Jude 1:9, we have to make sure that we do not misuse our authority in Christ. In all things, we have to be led by the Holy Spirit. God may not give us permission to pray against certain powers, such as territorial spirits. Instead, we can pray that God will Himself intervene to deal with these evil forces. God has given us power over all forces of the devil (Luke 10:19), but we have to use this power under the leading of the Holy Spirit.

"Father, I repent for any way I have misused my authority in Christ and prayed wrongly. By Your mercy, deliver me from the negative consequences of these prayers. Holy Spirit, make me aware and correct me whenever I pray amiss." (Proverbs 4:7, 14:12)

Opened Doors

"Call to Me, and I will answer you, and show you great and mighty
things, which you do not know." – Jeremiah 33:3

Certain spiritual warfare occurs in our lives as a result of
sins that have not been confessed. In fact, some of the
attacks I experienced in the dreams were because the devil
had obtained rights to attack me because of past sins. For
instance, when God was delivering me past sexual sins, many
of those evil forces were manifesting in my dreams.
Nevertheless, God allowed them to manifest so that I would
realize that a door was open in my life that was welcoming
these forces.

I had to ask the Holy Spirit to reveal to me the source of
the issue that was allowing the enemy to influence my life. In
times of spiritual warfare, we cannot fight an enemy we do
not know. We have to ask the Holy Spirit to lead us and to
reveal all truth to us so that we will be able to pray effectively
against the correct adversary.

God Is with You

"When you pass through the waters, I will be with you; And
through the rivers, they shall not overflow you. When you walk
through the fire, you shall not be burned, nor shall the flame scorch
you." – Isaiah 43:2

During times of strong spiritual warfare, I became angry with God. I could not understand why He was allowing me to endure so much pain. This was a time when I felt so much warfare in my life. People close to me were attacking me because I had become a Christian. In addition, I was experiencing a lot of attacks in my sleep, which left me sleepless for many nights. Sometimes, these attacks would last for weeks. I would cry out to God in prayer, "Please stop this warfare!" Nevertheless, it seemed like He was silent and not present with me through the battle. God's allowing His beloved child to endure so much was very difficult for me to believe.

Satan does everything for us to believe that God is not with us when we go through difficult times, but the truth is that God will never leave us nor forsake us. When we walk through fire, God is there with us, walking with us and comforting us (Psalm 23:4). Only His presence in our lives prevents the enemy from prevailing over us.

Nothing can separate us from the love of God—not persecution, trials, attacks upon attacks, nothing! (Romans 8:38, 39). God will forever love us, and nothing can separate us from our Savior. He watches over us all the time because we are the apple of His eye. The spiritual warfare is simply for a season and will not last forever. God's ways are not our ways, and there is a greater purpose as to why He allows us to endure certain things. At the end, He knows that we will grow stronger in Him and more able to help others through their trials.

Prayers for Spiritual Warfare

1) *Holy Spirit, reveal to me the source and solution of every spiritual warfare I am going through and give me a receiving heart to accept Your revelation and truth, in Jesus' name. (John 14:26)*

2) *Pray in the Holy Spirit for as long as you feel led.* (If you cannot pray that way but desire to, ask the Holy Spirit to baptize you with this gift of speaking in the Holy Spirit/tongues. Do not give up; keep on asking until you receive it).

3) *I cover my body, soul, spirit, family, friends, helpers of destiny, relationships, finances, health, home, vehicles, career, ministry, and possessions in the blood of Jesus. (Revelation 12:11)*

4) *You, evil trespasser of my life* [mention name(s) of the evil force(s) troubling you], *Christ has triumph over you, and you are defeated! I come against you, in Jesus' name. I bind and silence you, in Jesus' name. (Colossians 2:14, 15)*

5) *Father, send reinforcement of Your elite angels to encamp around me and my household at all times, and to bind and silence every oppressor of our lives, in Jesus' name. (Psalm 34:7)*

6) *Father, raise intercessors to pray for me by the leading of Your Holy Spirit, in Jesus' name.* (Acts 12:5)

7) *Holy Ghost fire* [repeat seven times], *incubate me and my household in Your fire, in Jesus' name.* (Hebrews 12:29, Zechariah 2:5)

8) *Thank You, Lord, for You are with me, and You will never abandon me. I am confident that you will guide me through this season and give me peace.* (Psalm 91, Psalm 23:4)

If you are going through strong spiritual warfare, I also encourage you to visit the Ransomed Heart Ministries' online page[12]. The site includes a list of "Daily Prayers" you can use to pray that I have found extremely effective.

PART THREE

All for a Purpose

CHAPTER NINE
Christianity Is Not Easy...

"I have told you all this so that you may have peace in me. Here on earth you will have many trials and sorrows. But take heart, because I have overcome the world." – John 16:33, NLT

While this victorious season of deliverance was occurring in my spiritual life, the enemy started using the people dear to me against me. The people who were closest to me began to despise me because of my faith. To my surprise, some of them completely disconnected themselves from me. I felt as if my world completely shifted before my eyes. I could not understand why my love for Jesus would bring conflict in my relationships. It was one of the most difficult seasons of my life. Nonetheless, through these trials, I learned what following Jesus truly meant.

My Family or Jesus?

After giving my life to Christ, it was like love at first sight. God had healed me from a broken heart and had filled me with so much love. Christianity seemed to me like heaven on earth, and having Jesus in my life made everything about life easier. At that time, all I wanted to do was to tell others about Jesus and how He had transformed me into a better person. I was confident that my family would also fall in love with Jesus and desire the same transformation I was enjoying in Christ. That a major change had taken place in my character was evident, and they seemed to enjoy this new person I had become.

Before giving my life to Christ, I used to be very argumentative and would often become easily angry or upset. However, after surrendering my life to Jesus, God was teaching me how to truly love and respect others, and my family could see that I had changed for the better. The things that once easily upset me were no longer affecting me. Instead, if I knew I had offended anyone, God would lead me to apologize for my wrongdoings to ensure that I was at peace with people. God had completely changed my heart, and I was excited to see Him change the hearts of those around me. In fact, at the time, I was the only one in my family who had accepted Jesus. Most of my prayer requests were about God's redeeming my family the same way He had redeemed me. Yet what I did not know then was that my family was not ready to receive Jesus as their Lord and Savior. On the contrary, as I grew in my walk with Christ, I realized that some of my decisions would actually cause a part of my family to separate themselves from me.

Most of my family members had grown up in the Jehovah's Witnesses faith but, over the years, some departed from that religion, while others remained. Nevertheless, a big part of my family was devout Jehovah's Witnesses. After becoming a Christian, I would sometimes follow them to attend Jehovah's Witnesses services. I wanted to please my family, and I thought I could balance Jesus with my family's religion. To add, I knew that if I stopped attending Jehovah Witnesses meetings, some of my family members would be hurt and potentially despise me for my decision. I did not want to feel excluded because of my love for Jesus. I wanted to be at peace with my family, and I did not want to be rejected by them.

Deep within me, I felt uncomfortable because I knew the Jehovah's Witnesses were not preaching the truth about Jesus and their belief about salvation was in contradiction with the Gospel. I felt like I had a battle within me to choose whether to fully follow Jesus or my family's religion. I was afraid of the consequences of my decision. I was yet to learn that I needed to be willing to lose everything and everyone in order to truly follow Christ.

"If people come to me and are not ready to abandon their fathers, mothers, wives, children, brothers, and sisters, as well as their own lives, they cannot be my disciples." - Luke 14:26, GW

I could not play pretense with my family or Jesus. If my love for Jesus was genuine, I had to let them know that I had decided to follow Him and Him alone. I needed to express to those around me how much Jesus had transformed my life. In fact, I felt deep within me that God wanted to make me His vessel in my family. He wanted me to stand for the truth in my family and not to pretend that I agreed with the teaching of Jehovah's Witnesses. God wanted me to make it clear to those around me that I was following Christ and could no longer do those things which were against His Word.

I knew that by making a radical stand to follow Christ, my family would distance themselves from me because they had been taught not to be close to non-Jehovah's Witnesses. Nevertheless, God's plan was not to divide my family but to use me to reconcile them back to Him. God did not want me to stop loving my loved ones because they did not yet believe in Jesus. He wanted me to continually pray for them and to be loving toward them—no matter how they treated me.

I must confess that it was a difficult journey in which I truly had to learn to trust God. I had come to understand that following Christ was not as easy as I had thought, but I knew that I had to follow God no matter what. My relationship with my family indeed shifted, and because of my faith, some family members even stopped talking to me. I had no idea how to balance love and persecution at the same time but that became my reality as a young Christian.

One incident occurred when I was still very young in my walk with the Lord. I tried to minister to a close relative by explaining to him why the teachings of Jehovah's Witnesses were wrong. However, that relative felt extremely offended by my behavior. I have to admit that, at the time, I had a lot of zeal for God but I was not using enough tact when preaching to others. In fact, I learned there is a proper time to preach to people and a time to remain silent while waiting on God for an open door to preach to others. I had ministered to that relative at the wrong time, which explains why he was angry at me. The worst part is that this close relative stopped talking to me for almost six months after that incident. I was very troubled by what happened, but that entire incident was a learning opportunity for me.

One major lesson I learned was that I did not have to impose my faith on my family. All God wanted me to do was to love them and pray for their salvation. Just as God had patiently waited on me to give my life to Christ, I also had to be patient with my family. I needed to preach to my family by the way I lived and loved them, and trust that one day God will lead them to Him. However, it was very difficult at first to understand why my family would despise me so much for following Jesus.

"Satan, who is the god of this world, has blinded the minds of those who don't believe. They are unable to see the glorious light of the Good News. They don't understand this message about the glory of Christ, who is the exact likeness of God." – 2 Corinthians 4:4

The enemy, Satan, blinds people and hardens their heart from believing the truth about God. In John 12, we can see that even some of the people who had seen Jesus and witnessed the miracles He had performed still did not believe in Him. The same things still occur today. Before giving my life to Christ, I was also blinded by the devil and unable to believe those who would minister to me about Christ. In fact, at times my friends invited me to their churches, and there, I would hear about the Gospel of Jesus Christ. Yet whenever the preachers gave an altar call to surrender to Jesus, I would harden my heart and not respond to the call.

I also recall a time when I insulted one of my friends, who was a Christian believer and praying for my salvation, and told her that she was a hypocrite. "You're no better than me," I lashed out at her. I did not know then that the enemy was not only using me to discourage her from praying for my salvation but also blinding me so that I would not receive the truth.

The same issue was now happening with my family; they were not only unwilling to hear about Christ but also unwilling to accept that I had surrendered my life to Him. As a born-again believer, God was now showing me that I needed to pray and forgive those family members who were persecuting me because they had no idea that what they were doing was wrong. Persecution is a strong word, but this is exactly how I felt after announcing to certain members of my family that I had given my life to Jesus. If that was not enough, problems actually intensified within my family— especially when they learned that I was giving ten percent of my income (my tithe) to my church.

The Jehovah's Witnesses was the prevalent religion of choice in my family. However, some of my family members had left that religion years ago because of bad experiences and their disappointment with the organization. As a result, some of them became very skeptical and disappointed about religion, which explains why it was hard for them to understand certain things such as paying tithes. To them, my church and pastor was using me to enrich themselves. This was a lie the enemy was able to plant in their minds because of their past disappointment with religion. They had lost complete trust in religion, and they simply thought my church was manipulating me.

I took the time to explain to them why I believed in tithing such as because I wanted to give back to God by helping spread the Gospel and support ministerial and missionary work in my church. Nevertheless, they could not understand my decisions and were convinced I was being completely brainwashed. For those family members who were still Jehovah's Witnesses, they also did not believe in tithing and simply thought I had completely lost my mind.

Nearly all my family was convinced that my Christianity had gone too far. Receiving these constant criticisms was not easy, and it truly felt like intense persecution, but I had made up my mind that I would follow Jesus—no matter what my family said or did to me. It was not easy, and oftentimes, I ended up very discouraged because, during that season, I could no longer have a normal conversation without my family attacking my faith. There were times when I would get angry at them, which is exactly what the devil wanted.

The same way the devil had used me when I was an unbeliever to discourage my friend from ministering to me was now the same way he was using my family to discourage me from loving them. In fact, every time we are praying for someone's salvation or ministering to someone about Christ, the enemy will try to stop us. That is why at times the same person we are praying for can suddenly become extremely hostile and oppositional toward us. That person is unaware that the enemy is influencing him or her as an instrument against us. Instead of retaliating in anger or discouragement, we have to stand strong in love and pray more fervently.

The devil wanted me to argue with my family and develop anger toward them. but the real battle was against him not them. In fact, what I was going through with my family was a spiritual warfare, and I needed to learn how to fight back in prayer to gain victory. In a dream, God showed me that the devil was using my family to bring discouragement in my life. In fact, the more my family attacked my faith, the more I would get discouraged, which is why I had to pray against that spirit of discouragement. I could not allow it to affect me or manipulate my loved ones. It may have looked like my family was behind the warfare but they were not the ones.

A real spiritual evil was trying to divide my family and blame Jesus for it. God was equipping me with the knowledge I needed to fight that enemy from the place of prayer. One surprising fact was that this spiritual warfare with my family was occurring at the same time as my season of deliverance. During my season of deliverance, I was growing in my walk with the Lord and learning to stand strong in the victory Christ has given me. I was experiencing tremendous deliverance and healing, and I was becoming more secure in my identity in Christ.

The enemy knew that one of the best ways to weaken my faith and my willingness to stand with Christ would be to use my loved ones against me. I thank God for giving me the spiritual discernment to recognize that the battle was a spiritual one and not a physical one (2 Corinthians 10:4).

Through consistent prayer, changes began to occur in my relationship with my family. They stopped attacking me because of my faith. It became like day and night. Some family members who were extremely against my becoming a Christian, later told me that they respected my decision and that they were happy to know that Jesus was making me a better person. The devil was no longer able to use my family to attack me because I stood on the Word of God to shield myself from discouragement. The fear and disappointment I once felt when I would talk to my family was gone. I continuously pray that God will lead all of my loved ones to accept Jesus and soften their hearts toward Him.

My Friends or Jesus?

"Do not be unequally yoked together with unbelievers. For what fellowship has righteousness with lawlessness? And what communion has light with darkness? And what accord has Christ

with Belial? Or what part has a believer with an unbeliever?"

— 2 Corinthians 6:14, 15

A French proverb says, "Show me who your friends are, and I will tell you who you are." While growing in my walk with the Lord, I began to realize that I could no longer relate with some of my friends the way that I once had. In fact, some of them were excited about the transformation that had occurred in my life, but they still wanted me to join them in certain activities I knew I could no longer do. As a Christian, I knew smoking, drinking, partying in improper places, having illicit sex, or even gossiping was wrong.

I had a strong conviction not to go back to my former habits. I no longer wanted to be a vessel the enemy could influence to do evil. God had enlightened my eyes and had delivered me from my former bad habits, I wanted to be a true ambassador for Christ—not a hypocrite. The issue was that some of my friends were not able to accept this reality. I was no longer cool to them if I did not follow them in doing what I now considered wrong. Clearly, my decision to follow Jesus would break some of my friendships.

The Bible tells us in 2 Corinthians 6:14, 15, "*what accord has Christ with Belial?*" Even though the Scripture was not yet totally clear to me, God knew that if I remained close to certain friends, they would negatively influence my new identity in Christ. Nevertheless, when I gave my life to Christ, I was still very attached to former friends, and I thought that our relationships would remain the same. The same way I had hoped that my family would accept my new identity in Christ, I had also hoped that my friends would accept me for who I had become. But many did not. In fact, many distanced themselves from me and were no longer interested in our friendship. I will never forget one particular night when it became clear to me that I had to let go of some of these friends.

One night I had planned dinner with a friend who had been my close friend for years. We had shared good memories, and I had hoped she would accept my newfound faith. She loved to talk about religion, so I was excited to share with her my new experience in Christ. Nevertheless, that night it became clear that a major shift had occurred in our friendship. In fact, to my surprise, the moment I mentioned Jesus in our conversation, she became very upset. I tried to change the subject when I saw her reaction, but she argued with me about my faith. She was unhappy that I had become a Christian, and throughout that night, I was unable to have a normal conversation with her. Even when I tried to talk about other things than God, it seemed that we could not agree on anything. I felt such a strong separation between us—as if a totally different person was sitting across from me.

I could not understand what had happened. In the past, we had spent most of our time laughing together and enjoying every moment we shared. It was the first time we had such a disagreement. I honestly felt this totally different person seated across from me had never been my close friend because so much hostility filled the room.

During that moment of great realization, something even more shocking happened before my eyes. While looking my friend in the eyes, I believe God opened my spiritual eyes. My friend's eyes were light-brown, but as I looked at her at that particular moment, her eyes seemed to be completely black. I actually felt as if her eyes were filled with darkness, and that awareness shocked me. For weeks, I wondered what had happened. I blamed myself for our argument that night because I wanted to maintain our friendship the way it was. Yet God made me realize a major truth that I could not avoid.

The last time I had seen that friend, I was an unbeliever. Most of my time spent with her was spent partying in night clubs, smoking, drinking, gossiping, stealing, and the like. As a new creature in Christ, I was no longer living in that darkness, but in light. The same darkness I saw in her eyes was the same darkness living in me when I was still unsaved. However, Christ had set me free from the power of darkness and had translated me into His marvelous light. Like

2 Corinthians 6:14 clearly states, light and darkness cannot fellowship with one another. God opened my spiritual eyes during that dinner to reveal to me that I could no longer remain close to that friend and some others too. We lived completely different lives, which is why I felt that she was a different person. The truth is that she had not changed from the last time I saw her, but I did. I still loved her dearly and fervently prayed for her salvation. However, I had to make it clear to her that I will not go back to my folly (Proverbs 28:11). I had to protect my salvation, and I could no longer allow my friends' life choices to negatively influence me. I never pushed my friends away from my life because I wanted them to see how much God loved them through me. Nevertheless, some of them walked out of my life. They simply stopped contacting me because my life was no longer interesting to them.

Looking back, I thank God for the grace He gave me not to run back after them. If their interest in me was only based on my doing what is evil, then our maintaining our friendship would have been destructive to me and also to them. Today, I still love them dearly, and I continuously pray for them to experience God's best for their life. I have no resentment toward them, and I long for the day I see them transformed into who God ordained them to be on earth.

Christianity Is Not Easy, but It Is Worth It!

Christianity was not the bed of roses I had imagined after giving my life to Christ. Standing for Jesus has been a very challenging journey, and I know it will continue to be. The persecution and rejection I faced from family and friends after giving my life to Christ was very difficult to swallow. During those times, Christianity felt more like a thorn in my flesh. In fact, I valued my friends and family, and I wanted to keep every one of them in my life. Yet a clear separation had arisen because of my faith. Tears were not enough to explain the pain I felt. I wondered for a while whether I had made the right decisions to follow Jesus, instead of keeping the peace around me. Feeling like a total outcast was not pleasant. Yet God made me to understand that things will get better if I trusted Him.

What I did not know was that God allowed that separation to occur with my family and friends so that I could rebuild healthier relationships with them and allow Jesus to be at the center of these relationships. God did not want me to hide my love for Him to others. On the contrary, I was called to shine the light and love of Christ in every relationship. God wanted to use me to transform the lives of those around me. God knew that many of my relationships had wrong foundations and expectations. For me to pretend to others that I was still the same old Sonya when I was not would have been unhealthy. The truth is that Jesus had changed me, and I had to trust God that one day my family and friends will see and acknowledge that change in me. To the glory of God, many finally did!

That journey was not easy, but it was so worth it! Seeing some of my family and friends draw near to Christ has been one of the best memories in my life. In fact, when one very close relative gave her life to Christ, it was like a dream to me. We had been extremely close for over a decade but after my salvation, there had been great friction in our relationship. She felt that I had been brainwashed by my church and would become extremely upset every time she saw me go to church or mentioned anything related to it.

I tried my best to stay close to her, but the rejection I felt from her was painful. One day to encourage me, God showed me in a dream that this relative would one day ask me questions about Jesus and give her life to Him. I woke from that dream excited but skeptical due to the present circumstances in my relationship with her. To the glory of God, fast forward about three years from that dream to exactly what God had showed me come to pass in my living room...

Over the years many changes had taken place in my relationship with that relative. She had accepted me for who I had become as a Christian and had even acknowledged to other relatives that I had changed for the better. She could see that God had transformed my heart, and she enjoyed our relationship much better. I enjoyed our "rebuilt" relationship too, and I felt that we had healthy boundaries, which allowed both of us to express who we were without feeling judged.

I never tried to push my faith on that relative because I strongly believed that only God can transform someone's heart for the better. The only thing I did on my end was to pray for my loved ones to have a personal encounter with Jesus. In fact, unless I felt led by the Holy Spirit or asked by others, I would not talk about my faith so that my loved ones would know my love for them was genuine—not because I wanted to change them. On occasion they would ask about God, and when these times came, I would lovingly share with them my faith in Christ.

I will never forget that afternoon in my living room when the dream God showed about that close relative coming to Christ came to pass! Over the years, God had placed Christians in her life to minister to her, and she had attended a couple of church services. Yet she was skeptical about churches but had developed an interest in learning more about Jesus. That afternoon, while we were talking about things completely unrelated to faith in God, she suddenly asked me questions about Jesus and the Bible. I was surprised and excited at the same time. I gently answered her first set of questions. However, she wanted to learn more, so she asked further questions. At that moment, the Holy Spirit brought the dream I had about her to my remembrance and whispered to me that her heart was ready to receive Jesus. I cannot describe the joy and excitement I felt. I was so excited that I was scared to ruin the entire moment and say the wrong thing. So I just prayed that God would take over and guide me. I can surely say that all the glory belongs to God because He fully prepared her heart for that moment.

She told me that she now believed in Jesus and was ready to receive Him into her heart. She wanted Him to change her life. I could not believe my eyes, but that dream came true. One of my closest relative who had once rejected me for giving my life to Jesus had now given her own life to Him! That moment completely erased the pain I felt from being rejected for my faith.

Christianity is not easy but is so worth it all! The hurt, pain, rejections, fear, embarrassment, persecution I faced for being a Christian was nothing compared to the reward of seeing my loved ones believe in Jesus. Over the years, more family members started believing in Jesus, and I can't thank God enough for transforming their hearts.

Another beautiful testimony is about a particular friend who stopped reaching out to me for almost two years. Because we had shared great memories together, I found it hard to let her go. I would often check on her, but she was not so responsive. She made it clear that she was no longer interested in being part of my life. She was an atheist, and she wanted nothing to do with Christians. She thought Christians were weak people who were simply being manipulated by their church.

God also encouraged me concerning her through a dream. In that dream, I saw her sitting in a very dark place, but suddenly she stood and screamed the name of Jesus multiple times. I knew God was encouraging me to continue praying for her and believe that one day she would surrender her life to Christ.

To the glory of God, she did. In fact, she reached out to me after almost two years of no communication. She told me that God had placed Christians in her life who had preached to her, and she now believed that God existed. She reached out to me because she wanted me to tell her more about Jesus. You have no idea the joy in my heart that day. When we met, she not only gladly listened to the gospel of Jesus but also surrendered her life to Him. I am forever thankful to God for transforming her heart!

Be encouraged because the persecution you may be facing from your loved ones because of your faith will not last forever if you do not lose hope. Be encouraged to know that God will change their heart for the better. Only believe. Do not let the present circumstances pull you down. Be faithful in loving and praying for those who persecute you and loving them, despite how they treat you.

One day, God will make that difficult journey all worth it! Be confident in this: God can soften and change the heart of any human being. With God, nothing is impossible! So be filled with faith and hope! I rejoice with you in advance for the salvation of your loved ones!

Prayers for Unsaved Loved Ones

1) I cover my body, soul, and spirit in the blood of Jesus (Revelation 12:11).

2) I claim my family and friends [mention names] for Jesus. I counter-petition Satan's claim over their lives, in Jesus' name (Joshua 24:15).

3) You, strongman, binding and blinding my loved ones [mention names] from believing the truth, I take authority over you. I bind and silence you. Leave their lives, in Jesus' name (Matthew 12:29).

4) I come against the spirit of discouragement sent into my life to weaken my faith, in Jesus' name (Psalm 11:2).

5) Father, uproot every resistance my family and friends have toward the Gospel. Remove their hearts of stone and give them a heart of flesh to know You. Make yourself real to them and draw them to Christ, in Jesus' name (Ezekiel 36:26, Jeremiah 24:7, John 6:44).

6) Father, send Spirit-filled laborers to minister the gospel to my family and friends, in Jesus' name (Luke 10:2).

7) I bring every conversation with my family and friends into captivity and to the obedience of Christ (Matthew 18:18, 2 Corinthians 10:5).

CHAPTER TEN
After You Have Suffered a Little While

"In his kindness God called you to share in his eternal glory by means of Christ Jesus. So after you have suffered a little while, he will restore, support, and strengthen you, and he will place you on a firm foundation." – 1 Peter 5:10, NLT

I took a three-year break from my career as an actuary to work on a business idea I had developed with a team. Our goal was to build a social network that would connect the startup community to facilitate exchange between founders, investors, and business vendors. When I became a Christian, we were still working on the prototype for that business and had not yet launched it. I was confident that we had a billion-dollar idea and that with God on my side, our startup would be a tremendous success. Yet less than a year after launching our online platform, we had to close it down. In fact, our team had reached a point where we could no longer meet the financial obligations of the business. Financially, matters had become very difficult for me. I had so much faith in God concerning that business that I left my actuarial career to focus on our startup growth. I was believing God for a breakthrough. All my savings and investments went into the business. However, marketing the business was more complicated than we had originally expected, and our team was unable to reach the success we anticipated.

Financially, I could no longer support the company nor myself, and I had no other choice than to close it down. It was a very difficult time, especially because some people found ways to blame my faith for the closure of the business. I had reached a point where I was embarrassed and felt like I was stuck in a pit. My personal bills were also piling up, and I was unable to pay them. I had no idea that I was about to go through a season of financial hardship.

I had reached a point where I was desperately looking for job opportunities to work again as an actuary, but doors were not opening for me to secure a full-time job. All I could find were part-time opportunities, which were unrelated to my field of studies and insufficient to allow me to become financially independent. I was living with family and friends, and I felt like I had failed at life. I could not even pay my phone bill or buy myself a new pair of shoes. I had shoes with holes in them, but I had no money to buy new ones. My finances had brought me to a place where I felt completely ashamed. It gave an opportunity for those who were upset about my belief in Jesus to mock me all the more. I could not understand why God would ever allow me to endure such embarrassment and mockery.

God, I Am Angry

During that season of financial hardship, I became angry with God. I started doubting God's plan for my life. I wondered why God was allowing me to go through financial hardship. I started running from God and dwelling in unbelief. I could not bring myself to trust that God was in control—even if my present circumstances did not look like it. I was at a point where I felt like I had given up everything to follow Jesus to no avail. I was angry at God. I blamed Him for the close of my business and for not opening a door for me to work full-time.

I started to doubt whether God truly had better plans for me. I asked myself thousands of questions about God and whether He was truly just. I wondered why He was allowing people to mock and persecute me, why He was not opening a door for me to get a stable job, why He was allowing me to look like a failure, why, why, and why!

During that time, the enemy used people to criticize me and to tell me things such as: "Where is your God to whom you pray to all the time? Why don't you ask Him for a job? Aren't you ashamed that people have to house you? What does God think of your situation? Does it bring Him glory?" I felt attacked all around because of my financial situation. I was angry at God because I simply could not understand why He would want me to endure financial hardship instead of simply giving me a job. I was disappointed in Him.

Never Get Offended with God

And when John had heard in prison about the works of Christ, he sent two of his disciples and said to Him, "Are You the Coming One, or do we look for another?" Jesus answered and said to them, "Go and tell John the things which you hear and see: The blind see and the lame walk; the lepers are cleansed and the deaf hear; the dead are raised up and the poor have the gospel preached to them. And blessed is he who is not offended because of Me."

– Matthew 11:2-6

Just like John the Baptist, I started doubting God. In Matthew 11, John the Baptist had been put in prison by Herod Antipas. There, he began to doubt whether or not

Jesus was truly the Messiah. John probably questioned why Jesus did nothing to get him out of prison if He were truly the Messiah. To answer John's doubt, Jesus pointed to the fact that miracles were taking place, which confirmed that He was the coming Messiah. The work of God was still going on, whether or not John was there. So Jesus told John the Baptist not to get offended with Him.

When afflictions arose in my life, I was totally offended with God. Instead of turning to Him, I turned away from Him. One of the weapons Satan used when I went through this season of financial hardship was doubt. He wanted me to leave my Christian race, and he was planting seeds of unbelief in my heart and mind. I started losing focus on what God was truly doing in my life because I wanted things to be done my way. God started ministering to me and showing me that Jesus never promised us that our walk with Him will be easy. Jesus, Himself, was persecuted while on earth, and the Bible is full of stories of people who had to endure hardship.

Job is the perfect example. His faith in God was severely tested as he lost all he had. Job was a man of upright character with God, and God made him very wealthy. Yet God allowed the devil to destroy his possessions, his children, and his health. No matter how tough Job's life became, he refused to give up on God. The enemy used his friends and even his wife to mock and accuse him. Job did not know why

God had allowed these afflictions to happen to him, but he refused to curse God.

God expects us to endure hardship as good soldiers of Christ and not be offended when these seasons arise in our life (2 Timothy 2:3-5). I could not get offended as God allowed me to endure financial hardship. God was not being wicked toward me. In fact, His thoughts toward me were always of good and not evil (Jeremiah 29:11). He had given me His Word that after I had suffered a little while, He would strengthen me and perfect all that concerned me. I had to repent to God for doubting Him and the plans He had for my life.

In the Bible, we see that Job also repented for questioning God's sovereignty and justice. Through his trial, Job held on to God, but he still questioned God as to why He had let all this evil happen to him. Job murmured against God because he was unable to see beyond his condition. Job had to acknowledge God's sovereign will and trust Him even with his unanswered questions.

Abiding in Him

"Abide in Me, and I in you. As the branch cannot bear fruit of itself, unless it abides in the vine, neither can you, unless you abide in Me." – John 15:4

Doubt represents a feeling of uncertainty about a particular situation. Thomas was one of Jesus's disciples who also had to overcome doubt. John 20:24-29 reveals how Thomas doubted when the disciples told him they had seen the Lord after Christ's death on the Cross. Thomas needed to see Jesus eye-to-eye in order to believe that He was truly alive. Jesus did not reject Thomas because of his doubts. In fact, Thomas always remained loyal to Christ and to His church. Thomas did not run away from God when he started having doubts. On the contrary, his doubts lead him closer to God as he sought answers to his questions. His questions were finally answered when he saw Jesus face-to-face.

Doubting can be positive if it leads us to ask questions and seek God for answers. In this case, doubt leads us to a closer relationship with God as we seek Him to get answers to learn more about who He is and His will for our lives. By asking God questions, we continue to abide in Him. Nevertheless, the Bible tells us that we live by faith and not by sight. God is a sovereign God, and He may never give us answers to questions while on earth. Jesus did not give an answer to John the Baptist as to why God had allowed him to be in prison. Instead, Jesus told him not to be offended by God's plan for his life. John had to trust God whether or not his circumstances were pleasant and whether or not He could see the hand of God in his life.

Doubt becomes dangerous when it leads us to run away from God and stop abiding in Him. We start asking the wrong questions, and we become susceptible to receiving answers from the wrong sources. Instead of trusting God's will and His answers, we want to impose our own will on Him. That is exactly what I did. As long as my situation was the way it was, I was unwilling to abide in the presence of God. I did not want to understand His will in this season of my life. In fact, I rejected the fact that, as a child of God, I had to endure hardship. The enemy was beginning to form strongholds of doubts in my mind, which were leading me to flee from God. Instead of seeking God's Word, I ran away from it. I was very strong-willed, and I refused to trust God. What I needed to understand was that God's plans for my life were always for good and not for evil (Jeremiah 29:11).

Demolishing Strongholds

"For I know the thoughts that I think toward you, says the LORD, thoughts of peace and not of evil, to give you a future and a hope."
– Jeremiah 29:11

In this season of my life, God wanted me to accomplish and learn many things. He knew that if I had a full-time job or even a business, I would not be able to know about or even fulfill His will for my life. He had a plan for my life that was different than what I was pursuing at the time. Nonetheless, my financial circumstances had completely weakened my faith, and it seemed that I accepted the lies the enemy was planting in my mind. Overcoming doubt became a severe spiritual battle. It seemed as if a stronghold had been built in my mind, and I had yielded to the idea that God was unjust toward me. I thank God that one morning, He sent His Word to deliver me from this mind battle. That morning I felt the Holy Spirit's telling me that if I persist in prayer against these doubts, they would go away. So just as the Holy Spirit told me, after persistent prayers, the doubts I carried slowly disappeared. From there, I was able to change my focus from my situation to what God was really doing in my life.

"I come against every mind-binding spirit, in Jesus' name. I pull down every stronghold of doubt erected in my mind. I bring every one of my thoughts to captivity and to the obedience of Christ, in Jesus' name. I decree that God has great plans for my life, plans of good and not evil, to give me a good hope, future, and expected end, in Jesus' name!" (2 Corinthians 10:4, Jeremiah 29:11).

What God was teaching me was that I needed to guard my mind and reject the doubts that were coming to my mind.

God wanted me to understand that those doubts were demonic, and I had no reason to doubt His faithfulness in my life. Once these doubts started disappearing, hope started filling my mind again. I started realizing that God was not against me, but for me.

Going through challenging times was indeed part of my Christian journey and not an exception. God was allowing me to go through this season for a reason. The issue was that I was asking God the wrong questions. Instead of doubting God, I needed to ask Him what He wanted me to do and learn through this season. I needed to trust His plan for my life and hold on to the grace He had released for me to endure this season of hardship.

Redefining Success

"But seek first the kingdom of God and His righteousness, and all these things shall be added to you." – Matthew 6:33

My financial position could not define who I was in Christ unless I allowed it to. I had no reason to be embarrassed for what I had or did not have. These were lies of the enemy, and he was using people to mock me so that I would feel bad about myself. I was chosen by God as His very own, and my values now came from being one of His children—not from my jobs, businesses, successes, or anything I had. Not having money in my bank did not make me poor. In Christ, I was rich no matter what my present circumstances looked like. Jesus became poor so that I may be rich. Whether I had a job, a home, a car, or any possession, in Christ, I was a king; I was heir of His possessions, I was chosen, and I was peculiar. Whether or not I could see it, this was who I was. God also wanted me to realize that He alone was my Provider—not a job or business. By assuming the contrary, I would only be limiting God. God can provide for us in many ways, and He can even perform miracles. In John 6, Jesus fed 5,000 people with five barley loaves and two fish. God uses our employers and people to bless us, but He is the ultimate Provider. I had to learn to redefine how I saw myself and separate myself from my situation.

For years, having a good job or owning a business was how I defined success. However, I had come to a point where I had none of these things, and that is why I felt like I had failed. God was now helping me to realize that success was never about the things of these earth but the things above. The Bible shares the story of the rich young ruler in Mark 10:17-27. Jesus asked this man to sell all of his possessions and give it to the poor. Jesus was showing him that the kingdom of God was not about the things we possess on earth. Yet this rich young ruler defined himself with the money and possessions he had. To him, these things defined his identity, and that was why he could not let go of them when Jesus asked him to.

We cannot find our identity in money. We can find it only in Christ! Any other thing we use to define ourselves is an idol. That is why, just as with the rich young ruler, we cannot be surprised when God asks us to remove the idols in our life. God is a jealous God, and He wants us to base our identity only in Him. In Christ, success is measured by how well we exact God's instructions for our life and set our minds on matters of the kingdom of God. Earth is not our home; God's kingdom is.

We have to set our hearts on heavenly things which have eternal value (Colossians 3:2). We cannot be so focused on things that will not transfer with us to heaven. Our needs, wants, expectations, and demands can cause us to be defeated in our walk with Christ and take our eyes away from the things that truly matter. My quest for a job and money caused me to forget the prize that really mattered. I became impatient and unwilling to follow the things of God. God was now showing me that I needed to shift my focus back to Him. I needed to truly understand and believe that seeking His kingdom, not a job, was far better than anything I could ever desire on earth. I needed to trust that, as I sought Him, everything else would be added unto me. God would make everything beautiful in His time as long as I followed His path for my life. I needed to shift my focus away from my own will and look up to Jesus, the Author and Finisher of my faith.

Success is about fulfilling God's will for our lives, not our self-will. Choosing any other route than the will of God means that we have formed an idol in our heart. I could not compare my life to that of other believers I knew. Some were working full-time jobs in the corporate world, but that position was because it was part of God's will for their lives. In that season of my life, working a full-time job or continuing on with my old business was not part of His plan for me. God was beginning to reveal to me His plan for my life, and I needed to trust that His will was far better than mine.

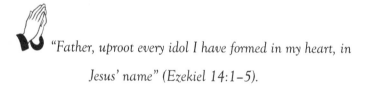 *"Father, uproot every idol I have formed in my heart, in Jesus' name"* (Ezekiel 14:1–5).

No More Comparison

"A peaceful heart leads to a healthy body; jealousy is like cancer in the bones" – Proverbs 14:30, NLT

One of the ways doubt entered my mind was through comparing myself to others. By comparing myself to what was happening in the lives of others, I started losing focus of the plans God had for my own life. God was actually doing great things in my life. However, my financial situation had led me to compare myself to others. I would look at my friends who had stable jobs or lived in their own home, and I would feel bad for not having these same things. I was losing focus of my own purpose by focusing on things that were not relevant for this season of my life.

I had to understand that everyone goes through different seasons, and for me to compare myself to what God was doing in the lives of others was not wise. I needed to guard my mind and guard my destiny. In fact, by comparing myself to others, I was drifting away from the plans God had for me. I needed to remove these distractions from my mind and refocus on what the will of God was for me in this season. I needed to revisit His Word and believe that His plans for me were not of evil, but for good.

I started praying that God would give me the grace to endure and to help me to refocus on what He had purposed for my life so that I would stop comparing myself to others. I made up my mind that I would no longer focus on what others were doing; rather, I would meditate on the great things God was doing in my life. With time and prayer, I was able to regain focus, and with the help of the Holy Spirit, I stopped comparing myself to other people.

A Grateful Heart

"In everything give thanks; for this is the will of God in Christ Jesus for you." – 1 Thessalonians 5:18

Thanksgiving is the most powerful weapon to overcoming doubt. When we go through difficult times, we start forgetting all of the great things God has done in our life. Instead, we start focusing on what He is not presently doing. Yet the Bible tells us to give thanks to God in all circumstances, whether good or bad, because it is the will of God for us. Thanking God is the best way to heal from pain. Being grateful takes our mind away from what we are presently going through to how great God is in our lives.

One of my mentors encouraged me to thank God for thirty-minute interval, multiple times during the day. The first day I tried, it was as if a miracle took place. All of the doubts I ever had completely left me, and I was filled with hope and joy. Thanking God actually strengthens my faith. I started truly believing that His will was the best for me. I started rejoicing in my present condition because I knew greater was coming. The more I thanked Him, the more I could see the bright light ahead. I was more willing to yield to His way and let go of my own plans, which were out of His will.

The strong-willed person I used to be was slowly becoming obedient to the will of God. I now make it a habit in my life to rejoice and thank God for everything, especially when I am going through a tough time. Thanksgiving is the best medicine to cope with difficult situations. It helped me to keep my eyes on Christ, the Author and Finisher of my faith. I had to learn that God was still God—no matter the trial. Being thankful was one of the best lessons God taught me. It enabled me to stop looking inward, but to focus on Him and how good He had been to me. God made me realize that I needed to develop a heart of gratitude. I needed to seek Him for who He was—not for what He could give me.

The Testimony Jar

"And they overcame him by the word of their testimony."

– Revelation 12:11

Complaining about what is presently going on in our lives and forgetting what God has already done can be easy. In fact, I had come to a point in my walk with Christ where I needed to understand that God did not owe me anything. I needed to make up my mind that I would be grateful and thankful to God, whether or not He took me out of this season of financial hardship. God wanted me to be thankful—no matter the season. God had already shown me so much mercy, but I had lost sight of it when I started going through hardship. I had to take the time to recount the testimonies that had already occurred in my life to encourage myself in the Lord. So I decided to create a testimony jar in which I included notes of my past testimonies. Indeed, if it were not for the mercy of God, I would have never come to Christ and would have ended up in hell. If it were not for the mercy of God, my past addictions would have destroyed me. God had been so merciful toward me and by creating a testimony jar, I was able to reflect and appreciate what God had already done in my life.

Sometimes, in the midst of our trials, we forget all of the miracles God has already done for us. My testimony jar has helped me to trace back all of the wonders God has done in my life. When we go through trials, the enemy wants us to forget how faithful God has been to us. Nevertheless, no matter what our present circumstances appear to be, God is good—all of the time.

After a Little While

"And the LORD restored Job's losses when he prayed for his friends.
Indeed, the LORD gave Job twice as much as he had before."
– Job 42:10

No matter how painful Job's suffering was, it only lasted a little while. God restored to him twice what he had lost. God did not allow Job's trials to overcome him, but God was able to test Job's faith through his afflictions. Job did not grow bitter toward family or friends who accused him. In fact, his friends thought that the reason why Job was suffering was because he had sinned. They were completely wrong, but God allowed them to attack Job to test his character. Instead of being bitter toward his friends who did not support him, Job forgave them and prayed for them. It was only after this that God restored Job's losses.

We can learn many lessons while we go through trials, and we need to focus on these things. Job did not depart from the precepts of God because he was enduring hardship. Job remained faithful to his faith. God taught me many lessons through my financial wilderness. These lessons not only tested my character but built up my faith in God.

CHAPTER ELEVEN
Lessons Learned in the Wilderness

"And not only that, but we also glory in tribulations, knowing that tribulation produces perseverance; and perseverance, character; and character, hope." – Romans 5:3, 4

I have learned that every time I go through a trial, God uses that experience to refine me and teach me a lesson. In fact, I believe that every trial in our walk with the Lord represents a test God uses to build our character and to help us develop more faith in Him. For a season, God allowed me to go through the wilderness of financial hardship. It was a true test of my faith in Him. Looking back, I know that God used that journey to produce perseverance in me and to build up my character. I believe the lessons I learned during that season were necessary for God to shape me into who He called me to be. God pays close attention to the development of our character and faith as Christians. God has great plans for us, but in order for us to fulfill them, He needs to refine us to make sure we can handle them. The word *test* in the Bible comes from the Greek work *dokimazo*, which means "to be proved and examined by trial." God can allow us to go through certain trials or wilderness to test whether our Christian faith is genuine.

Will we back out of His plan and purpose for our life when challenges arise and life gets hard? The parable of the sower in Luke 8:13 explains that the faith of some people is not truly genuine as in times of temptation they fall away from God. Trials should not cause us to run *away* from God but run *to* Him. Trials are tests of our Christian faith, and God uses them to build us up. Going through financial hardship was a difficult trial of my faith but a truly humbling experience. I grew so much during that trial that I now thank God for going through it.

Jesus also experienced trials, in which His faith was tested. He is an example we can follow when we also go through trails. Jesus went through the wilderness for forty days, and during that time, He was tempted by Satan. Satan knew Jesus was hungry, so he tempted Him with food. He knew Jesus was weak physically, so he tempted Him with power. God is not the one who tempts us; the devil is. Yet God can allow temptations to arise to test our character. We can see through the temptation Jesus went through that His faith in God was truly genuine. Jesus is the perfect example for us to follow. He has shown us through His actions that there is no trial or temptation that we cannot overcome.

Other great men and women also stand as examples for us such as Abraham who trusted God even when asked to sacrifice his only son. Like Jesus and Abraham, we have to pass our tests of faith in order to move up to our next level. God cannot take us to certain levels in our life if we do not pass certain tests. In fact, failure to past our tests only extends our time in the wilderness, which can turn out to be longer than what God originally intended.

God tested the Israelites' character in the wilderness, but they failed their exam by their constant grumbling and unbelief. Their lack of faith in God caused them to wander for forty more years in the wilderness until the unbelieving generation died off. This account proves that a pruning takes place in the wilderness. Through trials, God cuts off from our lives the things that weaken our faith and tampers with our character. Nevertheless, it is our choice to accept trials when they come and learn from them or to wander away from God. For me to understand how God was molding me through that wilderness season in order to come out of it victorious was crucial.

Humility

"Before honor is humility." – Proverbs 18:12

The first lesson God taught me in the wilderness was humility. I have to confess that I used to be prideful. I actually did not know I was prideful until I realize it was a challenge for me to seek help from others. When I started having financial challenges, I was embarrassed to tell others because I did not want them to look down on me. This attitude was prideful. I had built an image of myself, and I felt that asking people for help would make me look bad.

God saw straight to my heart, and my problem with pride became the first area He addressed in my life. I recall when I first told one of my mentors that I was struggling financially. She was surprised that I had kept the matter a secret for so long and told me straight up that I needed to be careful of being prideful because it would be a challenge in my walk with the Lord. She spoke to me in love, so I was not hurt by her words; on the contrary, I felt convicted in my spirit to deal with this area of my life. That God wanted me to pass the test of humility became clear to me. Actually, that was not the first time someone had told me to beware of pride.

One of my business partners prior to closing the business was a close friend of mine. She had helped me grow in my walk with the Lord and was a great blessing in the business. A particular incident occurred while we were working together that brought her concern about my character.

She had noticed that I was getting used to doing everything in the business on my own—even tasks that were part of her role as a partner. At the beginning she thought that passion for the business was motivating me to work so hard, until she realized that it could be pride. In fact, one day after sharing her concerns with me, I became angry and said, "My work is superior to yours; I do not trust you to do certain tasks." What I said was not the truth since she was excellent at fulfilling her role as a partner, yet pride was beginning to influence my behavior and speech. She was really offended by my comment, but she gracefully forgave me and never mentioned it again.

God was not done dealing with me. God knew I had developed pride in thinking that I don't need help from others and that I can achieve things on my own. He had sent my business partner to warn me, but I refused to listen. Well, my financial wilderness became the perfect opportunity for God to work on my character and to help me develop humility. As I have already mentioned, when my business closed down, I no longer had money and things got really tough. I was struggling to even pay for my phone bill. I prayed for provisions, and I knew God heard every prayer, but I believe God was testing me. God did not answer my prayers the way I thought He would. Instead of blessing me with a job, He used people to help me.

I never thought a day would come when I would write a letter to ask for money from my church, but that day came. God used my family and church to give me clothes, food, and money. I would have never thought that I would experience so much hardship and that I would have to rely on the help of others as much as I did. Nonetheless, I knew God was teaching me humility. I learned through the process not to despise the help of others. The truth is that I had no other choice, so pride had to leave and humility had to set in.

God provided for my needs by using people to bless me. This experienced humbled me and helped me to appreciate the help of others. It also helped me to be more teachable as I began to see that God could speak through others to help me grow. Quite interestingly, also in that season God brought key mentors in my life, or should I say helpers of destiny, who taught me about the ministry of prayer, inner healing, and deliverance. God probably knew that I had to learn humility prior to my encounter with them so I would be humble enough to receive instructions and knowledge from them. Looking back, I thank God for using this financial trial to humble me the way He did. This trial was one of the best gifts He gave me as a Christian.

Patience

Another major lesson God taught me in the wilderness was patience. Being patient was the hardest discipline I ever had to learn. I never thought I had a problem with patience until I truly had to be patient. God's ways are not our ways, and His thoughts are not our thoughts. God does not work according to our timing. I had to learn to trust in God's timing—not mine. I had to endure patiently and trust that His timing was better than mine. Indeed, God would make everything beautiful in His time. A thousand years in our sight is like a day with the Lord.

My plans were to secure a stable job that would enable me to get my own place and others things I wanted in life. God was providing for all that I needed at that time, but not all that I wanted. God was not opening the doors for me to work full-time. No matter where I was applying, doors were not opening for me to work there. My search became frustrating, and one day while praying, God gave me the following Scripture as an answer to my frustrations:

"For you have need of endurance, so that after you have done the will of God, you may receive the promise."

– Hebrews 10:36

God wanted me to be patient and seek His kingdom first. I was focused on my secular career, but God had better plans in mind. God used the time in which I was unemployed to reveal to me His purpose for my life. God taught me about deliverance and inner healing, which helped me overcome a lot of pain from my past. In fact, I wrote a major part of this book during the time I waited on God for a stable job. Even though I was excited about my spiritual growth, I had grown impatient of relying on others.

One amazing woman from my church had opened her home to me and had allowed me to stay with her for free, which was a true sign of God's favor. I finally had my own room, and I truly felt at peace there. Nevertheless, I had reached a point where I was tired of living with people, and I wanted to have my own place. God was meeting me at the point of my needs, but there were other things that I wanted to do or buy, which I could not afford. God did not think these things were necessary for the moment because He wanted me to focus on fulfilling His present will. But I had grown impatient of relying on people. I had to pray that God gave me the grace to be patient, even if I disliked my present circumstances.

One of the most beautiful stories about patience I learned

was during a time when I had a breakdown. A believer shared this story to encourage me. She told me that just as I had prayed and was waiting on God, other people had done the same. In fact, after I had prayed, I had to wait in line. Others who had been waiting longer than I had were ahead of me in line. God was answering their prayers because their time of waiting in line had ended.

In other words, there is a season for answered prayers, and I had to wait for my season—just like others had waited for theirs. Some prayers are answered immediately, but for others, we have to wait in line. That story really ministered to me at a time when I needed it the most.

God was truly perfecting things concerning me, but my impatience was blinding me from seeing the great things God was already doing in my life. God had better plans for me than working at a full-time job, and He needed me to be patient. I needed to refocus my thinking on what God wanted me to complete in this season so that I would be able to move to my next level. Through these trials, God was slowly developing the fruit of patience in me. Little by little, I stopped trying to force my ways on Him, and He gave me the grace to wait patiently.

Contentment

"Now godliness with contentment is great gain." – 1 Timothy 6:6

Contentment is "the state of being satisfied with what we have"—whatever that is. The apostle Paul defined it well in Philippians 4:11-12, when he explained that he had learned to be content in every situation, whether he was well-fed or hungry.

I will personally never forget how God taught me about contentment. In fact, I needed to learn this important lesson in order to stop wanting the things God did not find necessary for me to have in this season of my life.

While I was growing up in France, fashion was everything to me. The environment in which I lived encouraged people to follow the latest trends and acquire things. As a result, I developed a very strong materialistic mindset from my youth. To me, there was no such thing as being content in not having things.

God knew that I needed to learn a strong lesson about contentment, so He allowed something very interesting and funny to happen involving my desire to get the perfect birthday dress. I had planned a birthday dinner, but I had no money to buy a new dress. I wanted to look nice, and I came up with an idea to get a dress. I took a collection of clothes I had and tried to resell them at a thrift store. Most of these clothes had been given to me by friends, and they were new; some still had store tags on them. I knew that I would at least be able to resell some of the items.

As I boarded the bus on my way to the store, I heard the Holy Spirit clearly telling me: "My grace is sufficient for you." I was startled by hearing that verse being quoted and I knew, from that point on, that God did not really want me to sell the clothes I had. Nevertheless, I went on to the thrift store to sell the clothes. When I arrived at the thrift store, the store clerk disliked all of the clothes I had brought and refused to purchase any of them!

Looking back, I laugh at what happened, and it is very clear that God used that clerk to teach me a lesson. In fact, this "birthday-dress" incident is how God began teaching me about contentment. God knew that I already had dresses at home I could wear to my birthday dinner. He knew that I did not need another new dress, and I would be just fine with the ones I already had. God was teaching me about contentment because He knew I would need it for this season of my life. That birthday experience marked the beginning of learning to be content with my life. The idols we crave are sometimes what's troubling us more than what we don't have. That birthday dress was an idol—not a necessity. The moment I let that idol go, peace finally settled in.

The Principle of Sowing and Reaping

"Give, and you will receive. Your gift will return to you in full-pressed down, shaken together to make room for more, running over,

and poured into your lap. The amount you give will determine the

amount you get back." – Luke 6:38, NLT

There was not a better season in my life for God to teach me about giving than in this season of financial hardship. In fact, it was the perfect opportunity for God to teach me about His kingdom principle on giving. When I had more income, it was easier to give because I still had a lot left after I gave. When my financial situation changed, I had less to give. Nevertheless, in God's eyes, what I had was enough to learn the lessons He wanted to teach me concerning giving. In the kingdom of God, giving is the key to receiving. In order to receive more, we have to give more.

Giving is the most powerful key to unlocking our harvest, and it can be in the form of our talent, our time, our money, or many other ways. Most of the time, our harvest is tied to our giving. Yet the less we have, the less we want to give. For me, my bills and problems often made me think twice about how much I should give. However, God made me to see that I had a poverty mentality. The enemy tries to influence Christians to be stingy because he knows the secret to prosperity is in giving. I had to pray to overcome the spirit of mammon (Luke 16:13), which is the anti-giving spirit that makes people unwilling to give. We have to surrender to the Holy Spirit concerning our giving and listen to His voice when He encourages us to give.

*Then the LORD said to Elijah, "Go and live in the village of
Zarephath, near the city of Sidon. I have instructed a widow there
to feed you." "So he went to Zarephath. As he arrived at the gates
of the village, he saw a widow gathering sticks, and he asked her,
"Would you please bring me a little water in a cup?" As she was
going to get it, he called to her, "Bring me a bite of bread, too." But
she said, "I swear by the LORD your God that I don't have a single
piece of bread in the house. And I have only a handful of flour left
in the jar and a little cooking oil in the bottom of the jug. I was just
gathering a few sticks to cook this last meal, and then my son and I
will die." But Elijah said to her, "Don't be afraid! Go ahead and
do just what you've said, but make a little bread for me first. Then
use what's left to prepare a meal for yourself and your son. For this
is what the LORD, the God of Israel, says: There will always be
flour and olive oil left in your containers until the time when the
LORD sends rain and the crops grow again! So she did as Elijah
said, and she and Elijah and her family continued to eat for many
days. There was always enough flour and olive oil left in the
containers, just as the LORD had promised through Elijah."*
— *1 Kings 17:8–16, NLT*

The story of the widow of Zarephath in 1 Kings 17 is the

perfect example of how our blessing is tied to our obedience. This woman had only a little flour left to bake her last meal for her and her son. After that meal, she knew that she would die since there was no more for them to feed themselves. With the famine in the land, and she knew she could not produce any crop to survive. Nonetheless, when Elijah asked her to feed him with the last meal she had, she was not stingy. She told him what her situation was, but she trusted his word that if she obeyed him, God would provide for her and her son so they would not die.

She obeyed the instructions of the prophet Elijah and fed him first with the remaining flour before feeding her family. She sowed a seed into Elijah's life, and that seed was all she had. God rewarded her obedience and faith by blessing her with an abundant supply of food. That woman was in dire need of food to survive. In order for God to release the blessing to meet her need, she had to sow a seed first. She had to take this big step of faith, and she had to trust God that her family would not die after giving Him all she had.

Through the story of the widow of Zarephath, God was teaching me a valuable lesson: the best time to give is when we are in need. It seems contradictory, but it is true. The seed unlocks the blessing to meet our need. Throughout my financial wilderness, the Holy Spirit encouraged me not to focus on myself and my problems but to give especially of my time and talent. At first, it was annoying because I felt my time could have been used in working at a full-time job, instead of serving in church or tutoring children in need. I was also paying my tithe, which represents 10 percent of my income—even though I did not have much to give in the first place. However, the more I started sowing seeds of my time, talent, and treasure, I began to notice a reaping effect. In fact, from the time I started becoming an intentional giver, my financial situation started shifting. My bills were not only paid but also major parts of my debts were cancelled. Even without a stable income, God was meeting all of my financial needs and more. During my financial wilderness, I was able to travel on a mission trip outside of the country without paying anything for it and even enrolled in a Christian business school program without paying any school fee. I could share many more testimonies of the like. God simply used people to bless me. Many of these people were not necessarily close to me, which shows that God was moving them to help me and not what I may have done for them. These people actually told me that they felt strongly led by God to help me and bless me financially. The giving was simply incredible! I received in return much more than what I had originally given. In fact, the more I was giving, the more I was receiving.

I was beginning to understand the principle of sowing and reaping. If it was not for this season of financial hardship, I would have never seen the hand of God move in my life like I did. In fact, I may have attributed my blessings to my full-time job instead of God. However, throughout that season, I could clearly see that the hand of God was working for my good and for His glory!

The Test of Our Faith

"But He knows the way that I take; When He has tested me, I shall come forth as gold." – Job 23:10

During an exam, the examiner is always silent. At times during my season of financial hardship, I felt like God was not answering my prayers and was silent. God was always there, but He appeared silent throughout the times He was testing me. Through this journey, I learned to walk with Him and trust that He had matters under control even when it did not feel like it. When the disciples experienced a furious storm in Matthew 8:23–27, Jesus was there with them—only sleeping. Just like me, the disciples had to grow in their faith and stop worrying during difficult times.

During times of examination, God is observing whether we are learning and growing in a particular area. Jesus went through that exam in the wilderness when God allowed Him to be tempted by the devil. He passed the test of humility, self-control, patience, endurance, and many more. We also have times of examination when the Examiner, God, seems to be silent, but He is there.

To prepare for our tests, we have to take notes through the wilderness and ask God, "What do You want me to learn through this journey?" We have to prepare ourselves by holding on to His grace, reading His Word, listening to testimonies of other Christians who overcame similar challenges, and allowing the Holy Spirit to shape our character to be more Christ-like. Through the wilderness, we learn to become teachable in order to pass our exam. The process also enables us to grow our faith in the Lord as we trust that He will see us through every challenge. God will never allow us to be tested beyond what we are able to handle, so we can trust that at the end of His examination, we will come forth as gold.

CHAPTER TWELVE
Before I Formed You,
I Knew You

"Before I formed you in the womb I knew you, before you were born
I set you apart; I appointed you as a prophet to the nations."
– Jeremiah 1:5, NIV

---

*G*od has called each of us to fulfill unique assignments on earth. Indeed, we were created for a purpose, and the reason why we are on earth is to fulfill it. Long before we were born or conceived, God knew us; He already had prepared plans for our lives. He knew from the time we were yet born what we were capable of achieving on earth for His glory. He thought of us as being valuable to His kingdom, and He had a great purpose in mind for us.

"But God has chosen the foolish things of the world to put to shame the wise, and God has chosen the weak things of the world to put to shame the things which are mighty." – 1 Corinthians 1:27

For some time after giving my life to Christ, I lived in shame. I wondered if God would be able to use me in fulfilling His purpose because of the mistakes I made in the past. I felt as if I had not lived a life that was exemplary for a Christian. I felt sexual abuse, addictions, pornography, rebellion, fornication, and so forth had stained my destiny. All these thoughts were lies from the devil.

The truth is we have all sinned and fallen short of the glory of God. Everyone has a past—not just me. Sin brought pain and shame into our life. However, Jesus came to remove that shame and give us a brand-new beginning. So if we allow Him, God can turn our broken past into testimonies and make us His voice to our world. It does not matter how much we think we have messed up in life, God can redeem those broken pieces to glorify Himself. God does not waste anything, He turns both the good and the ugly parts of our lives into beauty.

In Christ, there is no shame! God never created us to carry the burden of shame. Sin brought shame, but Jesus took it away! The devil always want us to feel bad about our mistakes and live in condemnation. However, in Christ, we are called to live in freedom; we are called to live on purpose. We are called to live free from shame and fear. God was not ashamed of the life of addiction and sexual bondage I lived because He had plans to turn my mess into a message. In fact, God had planned to use my life story to minister to others who have gone through similar circumstances.

God knew that many people in bondage needed to hear my message. Women who have been sexually abused needed to hear my message. Heartbroken people needed to hear my message. There were men and women addicted to pornography who needed to hear my message. People on the verge of committing suicide needed to hear my message. They needed to hear that there is a God who heals, delivers, set frees, transforms and restores. We all have a message that God will use to draw people to Himself. That message is central to our purpose on earth.

God's Purpose Is the Best

"For I know the plans I have for you," declares the LORD, *"plans to prosper you and not to harm you, plans to give you hope and a future." – Jeremiah 29:11, NIV*

God's purpose for our life is the ultimate best. It makes total sense since He is the One who created us. He knows what we are made of better than we know ourselves. The

Bible says in Ephesians 1:4 that God chose us before the creation of the world, which is how long He has known us. The length of time He has known us far exceeds how long we have known our own selves. God knows the end from the beginning, and He can see the best route ahead of us. The assignment God has for our life is far bigger than we can imagine. Our purpose on earth is bigger than simply earning a living for ourselves. God has purposed to use us to transform lives and make a true impact in our world. He wants us to bring many to the saving knowledge of Christ so that they would be made whole and experience God's best for their lives.

Until we align ourselves with God's plan and purpose, we will always feel a void deep within us. It will be like living a defeated life and chasing after things that do not truly matter. I know how that feels, which is why I was extremely depressed before giving my life to Christ. I knew that I had a destiny to fulfill, but I was wasting away my life. I believe the Scripture *"deep calls unto deep..."* in Psalm 42:7 refers to the deep purpose of God's calling into the deepest part of our life for expression. Until we align ourselves with our purpose, there will always be a void in us. I remember when feeling that deep void within me that I was called to something bigger, but I was too weakened by bondages and depression to rise to that level. I praise God for Jesus who came to earth to help us rise to the level God purposed for our lives. In Christ, we no longer have to live depressed, discouraged, down, or with that void. In Christ, we are called to live on purpose, which is the only way to finding real fulfillment on earth. Yet this does not mean that difficulties, troubles, wildernesses will not arise in our fulfillment of purpose. Jesus told us that on earth, just like what He experienced, we will have challenges. However, the trials of life we experience are all part of God's plan to align us with His purpose and mature us as Christians.

My Wilderness Lead Me to His Purpose

Visualizing purpose when I went through financial challenges was extremely difficult for me. My focus was on my problems and my bank account, and I felt God was absent. God was not only very present in my life, but He was also making sure that I discover my purpose during that season of my life. At the beginning, I could not understand why God was not opening a door for me to have a stable, full-time job. I knew nothing was too difficult for God and that it was in His power to give me any job I wanted. Yet, He was not moving as I wished. The issue I had was that I was too carried away by my circumstances. In fact, the moment I shifted my focus on God and away from my problems, things became very clear to me.

I spent most of my life thinking that fulfilling purpose was related to financial prosperity, but I was wrong. Purpose has nothing to do with money but all to do with God and His kingdom. My wilderness not only helped me to shift my view on purpose, but it enabled me to discover it. I had to go through what I went through so that I could align myself with God's plan and purpose for my life.

I clearly recall the day when I felt God's telling me that He did not want a full-time job to interfere with what He was doing in my life. All along I thought God was doing nothing for me, when truly He was working miracles. So much amazing transformation took place during that financial wilderness. In fact, in that wilderness I learned how to hear God's voice, I uncovered my identity in Christ, and I experienced tremendous inner healing and deliverance. Also during that wilderness journey, I connected with major helpers of destiny (mentors) who sowed many seeds of love and wisdom into my life. Finally, during that wilderness time, I wrote the majority of this book. I thought my life had no meaning in the wilderness when, truly, I was fulfilling purpose. The transformation God worked in my life during my financial wilderness was instrumental to positioning me with His purpose.

That wilderness looked like a curse when it was truly a blessing. A full-time job at that time would have only been a distraction and a time waster. In fact, I had the wrong view on purpose. I thought having a full-time job meant having a purpose, but that was not a true perception. Many people with jobs have yet to discover and fulfill their purpose. That financial wilderness helped me shift my view on what it truly meant to live on purpose.

We sometimes wonder why God allows us to go through difficult times, but we are simply asking the wrong questions. We have to look at our circumstances through His lenses. Challenges would not look as bad if we simply asked God the right questions: "What are You trying to teach me in this season? What transformation are you doing in me? How is this trial aligning me to my purpose?" The wildernesses we go through in life may be so ugly and difficult that we feel purposeless in them. Yet they have an interesting way to bring out the best in us and lead us to fulfilling exactly what's best for us.

God's Purpose Is Conditional

The fulfillment of God's purpose in our life is conditional on our agreement. God is so good that He gave us free will to choose. God never wanted us to be robots who simply follow His instructions. He always wanted us to have a choice as to whether or not we would follow Him. God does not force us to fulfill His purpose. All God does is guide us toward what

He believes is best for us. In fact, He wants us to realize for ourselves that His plans are far better than any others, which is why He gave us free will. Unfortunately, despite of God's guidance, what has caused some to miss out on purpose are the idols they placed above God.

"Ephraim is joined to idols, Let him alone." – Hosea 4:17

The tribe of Ephraim was favored of God. As we can see in Genesis 48, Jacob gave Ephraim instead of the firstborn Manasseh the greater blessing. In the story of Hosea, *Ephraim* was another name for "Israel," the Northern Kingdom, as it was the most powerful of the ten tribes of the north. However, Ephraim had forgotten its spiritual heritage and had sold out to idols. As it is said in Hosea 4:17, Ephraim became joined to idols.

An *idol* is "anything that is contrary to God's purpose for our life." We can turn people or things into idols if we give them greater priority than God. Ephraim was favored by God above other tribes but later decided to go out of the will of God to serve idols. God told Hosea to leave the nation of Ephraim alone to reap the fruits of her perverse choices and idolatry.

God does not force us to follow His purpose. He may strive with us for some time but may later decide to leave us to our idols if we persist. A full-time job could have become an idol if I did not yield to God's leading for that season of my life. In fact, I knew at the time that I was called to write this book and learn from the mentors God had placed in my life. That season of my life could have been the only time available for me to achieve those goals. Failure on my part to recognize the purpose of that time and season would have made me miss out on God's best. God had made every provision to meet my needs, and I did not need a full-time job. Nevertheless, God left me with the choice: follow His leading or my idols. No matter my decision, it would not have affected God's purpose because He could have used someone else to write this book and achieve what He was calling me to do. Yes, the truth is that God's purposes will always be fulfilled whether or not we decide to be part of them.

The LORD of hosts has sworn, saying, "Surely, as I have thought, so it shall come to pass, and as I have purposed, so it shall stand."
– Isaiah 14:24

We are not indispensable to God; we can be replaced. In 1 Kings 19, Elijah thought that he was the only prophet left who was still faithful to God. However, God told him that He had reserved seven thousand prophets in Israel who did not bow down to Baal. Elijah was indeed favored of the Lord among the many prophets, but he was not the only one. He could have been replaced.

God's purpose for Samson was to use him to deliver the Israelites from the hands of the Philistines. Samson's disobedience did not stop God from fulfilling this purpose. In fact, God ended up using David to completely crush the Philistine opposition. God has a specific purpose He wants us to fulfill on earth, but if we decide to disagree with it and reject it, God will replace us and choose someone else to fulfill it. Nothing can get in the way of God's purpose—not even us. I pray that God will help us to come to alignment and agreement with His purpose. I also pray that we never make wrong decisions like Samson that would prevent us from living the abundant life Jesus has for us!

How I Discovered My Purpose

I knew from a very young age that I was called to fulfill something very special on earth. In fact, I have always longed to understand the purpose of my life. I believe God has planted a seed of purpose within each and every one of us. I recall times in primary school when I would look and stare at the sky for hours, longing to understand why I was on earth. Purpose was calling from deep within me for expression. Yet it was only after giving my life to Christ that I was able to grasp what that purpose was. In fact, I believe only God, our Creator, knows what our true purpose is.

"But the manifestation of the Spirit is given to each one for the profit of all: for to one is given the word of wisdom through the Spirit, to another the word of knowledge through the same Spirit, to another faith by the same Spirit, to another gifts of healings by the same Spirit, to another the working of miracles, to another prophecy, to another discerning of spirits, to another different kinds of tongues, to another the interpretation of tongues."

– 1 Corinthians 12:7–10

My discovery of purpose started with discovering my spiritual gifts. A spiritual *gift* is *a supernatural ability given by the Holy Spirit to fulfill God's purpose on earth*. Spiritual gifts are different than natural talents. Natural talents are usually inherited, based on our surroundings, or endowed by God. These natural talents are developed as we grow, and they help direct us in choosing a career or hobby. Spiritual gifts, however, are given to us at the time of our salvation to fulfill God's purpose on earth. These gifts mature as we grow in our walk with the Lord, and they are centered on God and His kingdom. They enable us to manifest God's divine presence to a world that so desperately needs Him. Our spiritual gifts enable us to express God's love to all humanity.

These gifts not only equip us in fulfilling purpose, but they also guide others in the fulfilment of their destiny. For me to understand my spiritual gifts in order to live on purpose was crucial.

One major spiritual gift God gave me is the gift of discerning of spirits. This gift enables a believer to know which spirit is influencing a situation or someone. In fact, this gift can allow someone to spot false teachings and prophets, and areas of deliverance in someone's life. I first realized I had this gift a couple of months after giving my life to Christ when I was invited to attend a "supposedly" Christian event. Even though I did not have much knowledge of the Bible, I could discern that what the person was preaching was not correct. In fact, because my spirit was not at peace, I could sense that this person was not telling people the truth.

The following morning, I reached out to mature Christians and explained to them what I heard at that event. They confirmed to me that what was preached was not true, and they were quite surprised that, as a young Christian, I was able to detect the falsehoods. They were actually the first ones to tell me that I probably had a spiritual gift, which enabled me to discern the truth. Most specifically, I believe God gave me the gift of discerning of spirits to equip me in the ministry of inner healing and deliverance.

I have personally gone through tremendous inner healing

and deliverance. God used precious mentors who invested years in helping me heal and gain freedom from the pain and bondages of my past. These mentors also have the gift of discerning of spirits, which enabled them to identify areas of my life that needed healing. Rick Warren, the author of *The Purpose Driven Life*[13], put together an amazing assessment called "S.H.A.P.E" to help a person discover his or her spiritual gifts. Using S.H.A.P.E. confirmed the different spiritual gifts God had placed in my life to equip me to live on purpose. As I began to understand more about my spiritual gifts, my purpose also became more evident. Still, not until God directly spoke did my purpose on earth become clear.

"Call to me and I will answer you and tell you great and unsearchable things you do not know." – Jeremiah 33:3, NIV

When I had finally surrendered to following God's will instead of struggling to obtain a full-time job, everything became more clear. In fact, up to that point, I had felt as if God was silent. Yet God answered a prayer so clearly that I will never forget. Jeremiah 33:3 became my reality the night I asked God a very simple question: why am I on earth?

God can speak to us in many different ways. Interestingly, God often uses dreams to speak to me, and through a dream,

God revealed to me His purpose for my life. That night in my dream, I saw someone in captivity who needed to be set free. I saw another person who was blind, in darkness, and needed to come to the light. I also saw another person being oppressed by the enemy who needed to be delivered. When I woke up, I had no doubt in my mind that I was called to minister salvation and deliverance to people living in darkness. God also led me to a Scripture that describes His purpose for my life:

"The Spirit of the Lord is upon me, because He has anointed me to preach the gospel to the poor; He has sent me to heal the brokenhearted, to proclaim liberty to the captives and recovery of sight to the blind, to set at liberty those who are oppressed."

– Luke 4:18

God has plans to use me to shine His light in very dark places and bring people out of darkness into His marvelous light. The years of inner healing and deliverance I received all made sense. In fact, I believe these ministries were central to my transformation as a Christian. I do not think I would have been able to grow in my walk with the Lord without receiving help through these ministries. I was completely broken when I met Jesus. Indeed, I was sitting in deep darkness, like the person I saw in my dream, when I met Him. God brought in the right people and resources to bring healing in areas of my life that had been broken.

Being sexually abused as a child had broken me, and God needed to put me back together, which He did through inner healing. For many years, I used to be in bondage to pornography, smoking, and anger. I had to break my agreement with those forces in order to gain my deliverance, which I did to the glory of God. God wanted me to pass the torch to others. He wanted me to guide others out of the darkness that once encompassed my life and into His life. That was major the call of God on my life. My testimony was His voice and light to my world!

"Father, my heart is willing. Reveal to me Your purpose for my life and redirect me if I have taken a wrong route. Help me to recognize, activate, and use my spiritual gifts so that I will be able to live on purpose, in Jesus' name" (Jeremiah 33:3).

Saying Yes to God's Purpose

For an entire week after dreaming of God's purpose for my life, I felt an internal struggle. The issue was that I used to believe the lie that living for God and fulfilling His purpose for my life meant that I would struggle financially. As a result, I was reluctant to fully trust God with my destiny. It was as if I did not believe His Word and that He would always meet all of my needs. So after making His purpose for my life clear to me, I struggled internally. I was concerned as to what my life would look like if I followed God fully. I was looking at my circumstances, and I was concerned that I will spend the rest of my life struggling. Yet those fears were not true since God never created us to struggle but to prosper.

Jesus did tell us that difficult seasons will surely come, but He promised that He will always give us the grace to overcome them. I had to shift my beliefs concerning God's goodness. I had to learn to trust Him and believe that what He had ahead of me was the best plan for my life. I wanted a full-time job so badly so that I could be financially stable. Yet what I did not know was that God was not only tracing the best path out of my financial wilderness, but He was also going to give me a debt-free life. I had to put my faith in God, despite what I was seeing in my life.

As I was waiting on God for a breakthrough, God was waiting on me for a response. Will I say yes to God's best for my life? That week felt like a long restless week, but God used a testimony to finally bring peace into my life.

In her book *Prepare for War*[10], Dr. Rebecca Brown explained how she made several covenants with God throughout her life. One of the covenants she made with God was vowing to follow God's calling for her life in the ministry of deliverance. As God saw her willingness to trust

Him, He used her greatly to bring deliverance to people all over the world.

As it happened, I read her book the exact week God revealed to me His purpose for my life. I know it was not a coincidence. In fact, I knew after reading her book that I had to give God an answer. I believe God used Rebecca Brown's testimony to help me put my trust in Him. I had to trust God that His plans were better than my own plans and that His ways were far greater and better than mine. All I had to do was to trust Him.

So at the end of that seemingly long week, I made a life-binding agreement with God. I told Him that I accepted His calling for my life and that I would follow Him wherever He took me. Things completely shifted in my life after I made this covenant with God.

God started positioning me in the right places to equip me for my destiny and with the right people who would help me in fulfilling my purpose. I believe that agreement fully realigned me with my destiny—not to mention that I got out of my financial wilderness when I started placing my full trust in God and not myself.

"Father, in Jesus' name, I covenant with You today, and I accept Your call for my life. Thank You for choosing me among the few and making me a vessel unto honor." - Sonya Rolande (12/29/14)

Right after making this covenant, God led me to enroll at Joseph Business School, a prominent Christian school that taught me how to prosper in business and ministry according to God's principles. I enrolled in that program without paying any school fees as a classmate felt led of God to pay my entire bill!

Miracles kept on coming… Right after graduating from that program, an amazing work opportunity came along. I am still working in that role as an actuary, and I am amazed at the miracles and wonders God is performing. I have seen co-workers give their life to Christ and get baptized. God has used me to minister inner healing, deliverance, and the love of Jesus to people at work who were heartbroken. God also used fellow Christian co-workers and me to start a Bible study group.

I do not consider this job a full-time job, but a God-ordained assignment. I also believe that God used this job to restore the years I felt I had lost working on my business and in the financial wilderness. An amazing testimony is that after only two years of working in that company, God increased my salary five times and to the level of people with many more years of experience than what I had. God performed this financial miracle to prove that He was indeed the Great Restorer. I was able not only to pay my debts but also use my income to finance the ministry work God was giving me and others.

God started positioning me in places beyond my wildest dreams once I placed my trust in Him. If God had released that work opportunity earlier, I would have turned it into an idol instead of using it as a platform to glorify Him. I thank God for shifting my perspective on purpose and preparing me for what He had ahead for me. I am confident of this: it is impossible to put God first and lose!

Living on Purpose

"I just wanted to give a testimony that God has broken my sexual desires stronghold. I have been celibate for some time now, but the desires were overwhelming. I would masturbate all the time, and I couldn't stop. Lustful thoughts consumed me, and it wasn't until praying with you that it was lifted. I feel a shift in me coming, I feel greater coming, I feel the Holy Spirit. Thank you for your obedience and for your anointing." – Anonymous Testimony

Testimonies are powerful weapons! I shared my testimony with this young lady (the previous anonymous testimony) of how God took me through inner healing and deliverance to free me from sexual bondages. I also prayed for her to experience breakthrough in areas she needed deliverance. To the glory of God, she sent me her testimony not long after!

The Bible tells us in Revelation 12:11 that we have

triumphed over the devil by the blood of Jesus and by the word of our testimony. Testimonies are indeed so powerful that they have as much power to save, heal, and deliver as the blood of Jesus. By allowing God to use my testimony, I have seen people experience miracles firsthand. In fact, over the years, God has given me many platforms to share His love and healing power to my world. Saying "Yes" to God to lead my destiny has been the best decision I have ever made.

Nothing is more rewarding than to make a positive impact in someone's destiny. I have seen God transform the lives of others by allowing Him to use me as His voice. Each time I minister to others, I feel deep within me a sense of fulfillment and a peace that I am living on purpose. In the same token, each time I am distracted and get carried away with the issues of life, I feel a void deep within me as if purpose is crying out for expression.

If you have not discovered your purpose, I encourage you today to ask God for it. You were not meant to live without a purpose. We are all called to live on purpose. I believe fulfilling purpose is a commitment to our world. Other people's destiny and eternity are dependent on our alignment with God's purpose. God's assignment for our life is bigger than just us, our career, or our loved ones. Some people will never fulfill their destiny if we do not fulfill ours. My life only began to have meaning when I understood this truth and aligned myself with God's plans.

From a rebellious child bound to sexual immorality, God redeemed all of my failures for His glory. He delivered beauty in my life and took away the years of ashes. If that was not enough, God not only gave me a fresh new start but also made me His voice to my generation.

Tears of joy and songs of thanksgiving will never be enough to express my gratitude. Thank You, Lord, for redeeming everything for beauty! May my life forever be pleasing to You, in Jesus' name. Amen!

Notes

1. The Holy Spirit is God (Acts 5:3-4), the third Person of the Trinity (1 Timothy 2:5), and He is the One who convicts us of our sins (John 16:8).

2. P.B. Wilson, *Your Knight in Shining Armor* (Eugene, Ore.: Harvest House Publishers, 2006).

3. Welcome to the family of God! Please, contact me on my Facebook page (facebook.com/SonyaRolande) so that I can pray along with you.

4. Chester D. and Betsy Kylstra, *Restoring the Foundations* (Pomona, NJ: Proclaiming His Word Inc., 2001).

5. International Society for the Study of Trauma and Dissociation. Dissociation FAQ's, http://www.isst-d.org/?contentID=76, retrieved May 19, 2018.

6. James B. Richards, *How to Stop the Pain* (New Kensington, Penna.: Whitaker House, 2001).

7. James W. and Michal Ann Goll, *Dream Language* (Destiny Image Publishers, 2006).

8. Damola Treasure Okenla, *Divine Connections: A Marital Prayer Guide and Tips* (XLibris, 2013). Kindle.

9. Joyce Meyer, *Battlefield of the Mind* (Brentwood, Tenn.: Warner Faith, 2002).

10. Rebecca Brown, *Prepare for War* (New Kensington, Penna.: Whitaker House, 1992).

11. John Paul Jackson, *Needless Casualties of War* (Streams Publishing House, 1999).

12. Ransomed Heart Ministries - Look up the 'Daily Prayers' at https://www.ransomedheart.com/pray.

13. Rick Warren, *The Purpose Driven Life* (Grand Rapids: Zondervan, 2013).

Prayer Points Index

Let's Stay Connected!

Did you give your life to Christ?

Do you have a testimony?

Do you want to learn more about the author?

Do you have feedback?

facebook.com/SonyaRolande

Made in the USA
Monee, IL
19 July 2022

99966229R00144